Little Bullies Can Become Big Jerks

Discovering the Effects of Jerkism in our Culture
With Help in Creating an Arena of Love
To Restore the Broken Hearts

Terry E. Lursen
"The Jerk Whisperer"

TEL Publishing

TEL Publishing

For further information, please email
terrylursen@gmail.com

Copyright © 2019 by Terry E. Lursen
Cover Design: Stephen Lursen Art
Published by: TEL Publishing

ISBN: 978-1-970094-06-0
Ebook ISBN: 978-1-970094-03-9

All rights reserved. Written permission must be secured from the publisher to use or reproduce any part of this book, except for brief quotations in critical reviews or articles.

Scripture taken from the NEW AMERICAN STANDARD BIBLE unless otherwise noted.

Scripture from the NEW AMERICAN STANDARD BIBLE © 1960, 1962, 1963, 1968, 1971, 1973, 1975, 1977, by the Lockman Foundation. Used by permission.

Scripture quotations are from the Holy Bible, English Standard Version ® (ESV ®) Copyright © 2001 by Crossway, a publishing ministry of Good News Publishers. Used by permission. All rights reserved.

The Holy Bible, Berean Study Bible, BSB. Copyright ©2016, 2018 by Bible Hub. Used by Permission. All Rights Reserved Worldwide.

Library of Congress Cataloging-in-Publication Data
Lursen, Terry E., 1957 –
little bullies can become big jerks: discovering the effects of jerkism in our culture with help in creating an arena of love to restore the broken hearts

Library of Congress Control Number: 2019952192

Acknowledgments

I want to thank my wife, Jane, for sticking it out with me for over 38 years. I have changed. We all have, and I thank God for you and for our future. I love you!

Thank you to my adult children, Jessica, Stephen and Cara, and Christian. You have seen the best of me and, unfortunately, some of the worst of me. God granted us favor, though, when He planted you all, because you all have grown to be the men and women of God that He delights in and we are forever grateful to Him.

Thank you to everyone who contributed to this work, to those who poured your heart out in the contributions and for those who read and reviewed the work...some of you many times. Thank you!

Contents

Introduction		9
Chapter One	Where Do Bullies and Jerks Come From?	20
Chapter Two	The Early Formations of a Jerk	34
Chapter Three	What Exactly Is a Jerk?	44
Chapter Four	Dealing With the Imperative	49
Chapter Five	Confessions to a Jerk	58
Chapter Six	The Very Worst of Traits	77
Chapter Seven	The Jerk's Confession	79
Chapter Eight	How to Stop Being a Jerk	81
Chapter Nine	How to Make Better Decisions	94
Chapter Ten	Thinking About How Other People Think	104
Chapter Eleven	Final Words	115
References and Citations		120

> *"Jesus called the crowd to him and said,
> 'Listen and understand. A man is not defiled by what enters his mouth, but by what comes out of it.'"*
> **(Matthew 15:10-11, Berean Study Bible)**

INTRODUCTION

The Land of Innocence
The Tale of the Ego Weed

The Sheriff of Innocence had been called out to capture all overgrown boys in the town that had gone out on an all-night binge of ego weed. Some of the boys had found the forbidden fruit in the far-far fields beyond the Dark Mountain.

They had been told many times to never go to the Dark Mountain, let alone the far-far fields that contained many things that they weren't supposed to touch.

Two of the boys that had already been caught were five times the size of a normal child. These two were in the jail cell that had been built for those who get out of order, but, until this particular day, it had never been used.

The jail cell was made of wooden bars with a large wooden barred door that had a latch on the inside of the door. Anyone could stick their hand inside the space of the door and lift the latch to get out. One of the overgrown boys had done just that by clumsily moving around in the pen and accidentally lifting the latch, thereby opening the door. Deputy Tee shoved the large, clumsy, overgrown boy back into the pen, re-latching the lock and told him, "Don't do that again!" The boys wearily moved away from the door ashamed of what they had done.

Deputy Tee asked the Sheriff why the latch was so easy to unlock and he said, "They didn't used to be that big. A normal sized boy would have never been able to reach that door latch."

The overgrown boys had not only traveled out to the Dark Mountain, they had meandered down the other side of the mountain. Their overgrownness was such that they looked like blown up blue balloons, filled with hot, puffy, ego-maniacal air. They had become rather gigantic in proportion to their normal size and they didn't have control over themselves. When they came back from the Dark Mountain, they felt different, but didn't realize how large they had grown and were basically out of control as they attempted to navigate themselves back to Innocence. They had been moving about the village like reckless blobs destroying their neighbors' homes and knocking over everything that was in their pathway. They couldn't control anything they did; kinda like large blue, rubberized balloons drifting through the village terrorizing everyone.

They had climbed the Dark Mountain to see what they could see. Then, they trudged the Dark Jungle to the far-far fields and found the forbidden ego weed. They not only touched it, but pulled the weeds up from the dark ground and ate their bellies full of the forbidden fruit. It caused them to feel really good, and they grew puffy and the more they ate, the more puffed up they became.

Deputy Tee proceeded through Innocence and upward towards the hillside when he heard the loud trouncing sound of horses' hoofs. To his dismay, a herd of wild horses was rampaging towards the village. He took cover among a circled grove of tulip poplar trees, four of them as each of them had two trunks. He slid between the trunks of the trees, along with some other boys that were assisting him.

The herd of horses were fleeing from a heard of bison that were closely catching up to them. They were destroying everything in their wake. The Deputy ran to the top of the hillside and saw that both herds of animals were running from the other two overgrown ego-weed filled boys that had not yet been caught. They had been out in the fields terrorizing the herds of animals and they had no idea the destruction that was occurring to the village as a result of their ridiculously, overgrown selves and their uncontrolled movements.

Terrific loss accompanied sadness, and was seen and felt by everyone in the village that day. Many people were left injured, homes were destroyed, and it seemed that it would take months, or even years, for the townspeople to recover from the destruction. The posse finally caught up with the two overgrown, puffed up forbidden fruit eaters and threw them in the jail cell with the others. They were kept there over time until the power of the ego weed dissipated, reducing them back to their normal size. From their view in the jail cell, they could see only a portion of the resulting devastation from the rampaging animals. Innocence had been destroyed by their own irresponsible behavior. They could not see how much pain they had created, nor how severe the destruction was, for their eyes could only see so far...

I share this story from the outset because it happens to be a part of why I'm writing this book. I try to help people and one of the ways in doing so, is pastoral counseling. I listen to people and try to make some sense of what is going on in their lives and use Biblical scripture as a tool in guiding us through the issues of the day.

I try to help people solve their problems from the inside out. This is not because I am any type of genius, it is, I tend to think, a result of my being a caring listener and a close examiner of my own imperfections, my own troubles that I created all by myself, and quite a bit of personal reflection as a result from an invasion of the Holy Spirit into my personal spirit that reveals just how careless I have been throughout the years. I have the ability to see what others do not, or, cannot, see about themselves. Helping others involves helping them to see the difference between a symptom and a problem. For example, if you believe you are an alcoholic, then, your alcoholism is a symptom. You medicate in order to relieve, or escape from the problem(s) that are either directly affecting you, or, are hidden deep within. I believe the Word of God is an incredible tool for answers to all of life's issues. I can listen to a person talk about themselves, or their problems for that day, without judgment, and, if they want to solve the problem, as their pastoral counselor, life coach or mentor, the Holy Spirit and I will typically have some inward solution to begin the process. Typically, I do not tell people what to do, I guide them along asking a lot of questions, so that they figure things out on their own...albeit, with the help of the Holy Spirit, the ultimate "jerk whisperer".

It is difficult to listen to oneself about your own personal issues and resolve them without going through a hoop of judgments and criticism about who or what you believe your problem makers tend to be. In our minds we like to blame others. Talking to oneself, simply put, is oftentimes debilitating because of the circles we find ourselves going into and round and round the mountain we go again and again. We are not our own best counselors.

And, speaking of counseling, let me tell you what this book is not. It is not a psychotherapists' view of narcissism, gaslighting, or any other myriad of personality disorders only diagnosed by a trained licensed mental health professional. The licensed professionals spend hours listening and giving people tests, reviews and more tests that are approved by the American Psychiatric Association to diagnose all kinds of disorders. In social media these days, too many people are led to believe that if such and such a person is exhibiting certain behaviors, then they must be a _____ and they, in their amateur psychotherapizing, (yes, I know that is not a word) can fill in the blank. This is not that. Amateur psychotherapizing really needs to stop. Social media does not give a person the right to label a person with a personality disorder...it's kind of jerkish, don't you think? That's acting like something you're not. Another thing that I have learned by experience in maturing is to talk about what you know and anything beyond that, remain silent. We can know what we know and to reach to our imagination, or someone else's imagination, for explanation is damaging to ourselves and to others. Although there are many similarities of the narcissist and the gaslighters in their abuse of their victims, we are strictly talking about the social phenomena of bullies and jerks.

Inasmuch, throughout my entire life, I have had quite a few problems. I have ISSUES. Many have been solved, yet others still lie in cue, waiting as it were, still there, still showing their ugly faces, and this, of my own doing. On more than one occasion my issues have let me know that they are still there and they are not going away any time soon. That is, they are not going anywhere from my within, without some extraordinary kind of help.

One of my problems, as we can presume from the title of this book, is not that I have had to deal with so many jerks in my life, for I have indeed, but, when I look into the mirror, I have to deal with the jerk I'm looking at in that moment. He simply doesn't seem to get it, at times, although, with much pain revealed through the law of reaping and sowing, he does see a glimmer of hope that there is light, life and restoration beyond the jerk that I know best and that person is me.

This brings us to the rationale of sharing the story of the Land of Innocence and the power of the ego weed. It was actually a dream that I had one night. Some folk look at dreams and say, "So what! It was a dream, it doesn't mean anything." Others look at dreams as some kind of spooky foretelling or post-something, or other, and try to make something out of it as supernatural.

I look at dreams in this particular manner...they mean something to the dreamer...only the dreamer. If I dream a dream, the dream is about me. There could be five, or more, different characters in the dream, but the dream is still about me. If you have a dream, the dream is about you. If you have a dream about another person in particular, it is your feelings/thoughts of how you feel, or think about the issue between you and that person, or how you feel about that person in general. I personally believe that it involves my unconsciousness bringing something to the surface for me to see. It could be something hidden, or stored deep within my unconscious and when it is brought to my attention in a dream, I have the opportunity to learn something from the experience. This is how Biblical dreams have been used in their context, to help the dreamer understand the dream about his/her self, the dreamer and the world in which he lives.

This dream is about four youths who disobey the laws of the land and go climb a mountain, travel to the far, far away fields and eat the forbidden fruit, the ego weed. Here is an inference to the dream of the Land of Innocence:

When a person feeds on their own ego, their puffed-up state of being gets noticed by others, but not necessarily by the ego-driven. This puffed-up person most assuredly lacks self-control in his words, tone, and behavior. The power of this out of control person, who we will call a bully/jerk is relatively unknown to him, and most especially the ensuing consequences that get created as a result of his actions. He sees what he sees in front of him and doesn't look back to see the destruction that occurs in other peoples' lives as he moves about in their midst. In this instance, in his recklessness to eat what was forbidden, his ego is elevated to ridiculous proportions and he is, seemingly, powerless to control his destructive nature for he does not care, nor, in this instance, is he able to. When he finally comes to himself, if he does, he can only see what he sees as in a glass, because the past is too far away to reckon with. Destruction is imminent when the jerk is in action.

You can make your own inferences here:

Since I dreamed that dream, that dream was about me. I have been the jerk. I have been a jerk, yet I am not a proud jerk as many jerks profess. I'm embarrassed at the things I've done. So many real-life jerks are proud of their jerkism and their ugly, mean jerky ways. I am seeing the results of my own personal jerkism and am ashamed of myself. That doesn't mean that I am weak, it means that I have a strong desire to stop hurting people and ruining my relationships. I want to change and I am changing. You do know that the verb definitions of to jerk is "sharp, sudden movements, to tear, wrench; to pluck, rip, seize, or tear". In a sense, the person who finds him or herself being a jerk is doing exactly that to another person. Yes, a jerk can either be a male, or a female. Being a jerk to others is to rip them; tear them in contempt; to seize them with a snatch of a comment, or an action to let them know that this jerk is in charge, if only for the moment of interaction. Jerkism knows no cultural, gender, or racial bounds. Jerkism has no limits to its tearing up other peoples' lives, leaving a wake of pain, loss and suffering. Snide, rude and off-putting comments about other people, most often breathed under the jerk's breath, become practice made perfect for the jerk who desires to make his, or her, derogatory comments made known, filled with contempt to the person of choice in the moment.

The jerk has no fear who they (and, going forth, we will use the term, "they" so as to not make a point that a jerk is only a guy of the worst sort, for I know quite a few female jerks of queenly proportions;) are a jerk to unless it's their boss, a person in authority who they may respect, or it's someone much bigger than they are in physical size, bank account, or recognized leadership ability. At that point, the jerk's demeanor can change rather abruptly to silence, or a smile, in order to kindly acquiesce...until another more opportune time presents itself to be a jerk to the lowly of estate.

The lack of self-worth oftentimes plays into the hands of the bully/jerk so much so that he/she has the need to bring others down to their level of self-worth through verbal abuse, name calling, spewing toxic tones and words upon those who are believed to be the "deserved" of all things toxic, hateful, spiteful, condescension, and, you get the picture...

The rationale of writing this book at this point in my life is coming from the many folk who I have counseled through the years. Many, many people are living hurt and wounded lives and many of these have been struck hard by the mean-spirited, uncaring, oftentimes, soul-less jerk. I was counseling an older lady recently and after much "speaking through" her pain, she finally landed in 1976 when she started revealing to me, through tears in her eyes, of the loss she has suffered much of her life as a result of her, then, jerk husband. She told me of the loss of her family, their son's youth in high school, her home and so much more. That man has no idea of the pain and loss he created by his own selfish behavior. The loss is still felt today.

The purposes of this book are numerous, the first of which is to bring light and illumination to what a real jerk is, but as Dr. Dan B. Allender, in his book, "The Wounded Heart: Hope For Adult Victims of Childhood Sexual Abuse," states, "Insight alone does not provide the impetus to change destructive behavior; it only creates a context for more fervent repentance. At its worst, an understanding of motivation may lead to fascination intrigue, self-absorptive introspection, and a focus away from issues of sin, salvation, and sanctification."[1] Because insight and illumination to what a real jerk is, is not enough, we will also pursue life in acknowledgement that many of us have been jerks at differing points in our lives and confess the destruction that the behaviors of the jerks in our lives have left behind for us to deal with. I have asked others to confess to the private jerks in their lives and contribute to this work so that we get a portion of what real jerkism is and the pain and loss they leave in their paths through life. In the process, some have recognized their own jerkish ways in the confession.

The second purpose is to propose something that is self-evident to some and completely oblivious to others and that is that little bullies are created and trained in the home by their parents, or, the lack of parents, and by their siblings. Bullying is learned at an early age by voraciously attentive children who watch and listen to how they are treated, how the parents treat one another and how other relatives and friends of relatives act in their home. Whatever happens in the home to a toddler is assumed to be perfectly normal behavior to that toddler...they do not know any better. If the child is abused physically, emotionally, or mentally, or they watch the mother, or father being abused by the other spouse, relative, or close friend, then, whatever is observed becomes learned and then exacted on others to their siblings, the daycare buddies, or the school playground. The anecdotes and stories given are living proof of this phenomena. What is said in the home gets repeated repeatedly. The parents of children must take responsibility for the angels, or demons, they create in their own home.

This book is geared towards better parenting. Better parents make better children. Better children make for a better future for all of us.

The adverse is also true, in that, when an adult is vacant, no where around, or, the adults are so inattentive, the child will learn from whomever, or whatever, is around. That could be cable TV, their friends and peers, music, video games, people on the street, gangs, etc. We all learn from what we get ourselves addicted to, or put copious amounts of time and energy into. If a child is left alone to themselves to video games, they become a real gamer, in reality. If the child is left alone, without parental, or teacher supervision, to be the constant companion to their peers, they will teach and learn from the peers. It is common sense, I believe, but it is also the answer to the question that the parent asks the child most often when the child has done something that is so out of character to the home environment and pleads with the child saying, "Where did you learn to do that?" Or, "Where did you learn to say that?"

The ending purpose is restoration for the abused victim, as well as, the bully/jerk that is out there reading this material and, hopefully, feels a compulsion to change. This will give that person an opportunity to see that their behavior is not laudable, but hurtful, demeaning and destructive. And, that they do not have to remain that person of contemptuousness, but can be healed and delivered from their nature to hurt others, subsequently, destroying relationships with people that they actually care about.

You see, the jerk practices and preaches their ways, sometimes unwittingly, all through life and eventually it gets to everyone they know. They sow their seeds in their spouses, children, friendships, work relationships, and people on the street. It is my desire for the reader to see him/her self in these pages. This is not a novel where there is the hero and the villain. For the most part, when we read a novel, we don't see ourselves as villainous and dastardly as the worst of villains could be, we tend to see ourselves as the part of the hero, the heroine, the savior, or the good guy. At least, it makes healthy sense that we would see ourselves that way. Not many folk who care about their relationships see themselves as villains in their everyday lives, yet, we do need to take a closer look at ourselves and, perhaps, we may see a glimpse, or two, of how we are actually the villain in that relationship that got crushed, crashed and burned, and then we think we buried the "deserving" relationship into the ground, and, yet, the other person who we have been abusing is still alive, but wounded, scarred, and troubled at what they did to deserve this unrelenting betrayal of humanity.

What has been your experience? Have you been the jerk, or the victim? Or, were you once or many times the victim, and now, you find yourself being the jerk?

Chapter One

Where Do Bullies and Jerks Come From

Based on a lifetime of experience in churchwork, church camps, youth outings, day camps, various opportunities to teach, pastoral counseling, raising three children of my own, and observing their friends and school experiences, I have a theory about where bullies and jerks come from. My theory is that little bullies who grow into big jerks learn what they learn at home from their parents who do what they do, or allow various types of errant experiences, in the home. The children learn what they learn and then take it to the streets, the school, church, or other settings. When I say, allow, there are those parents who allow their children to watch R rated movies, television, and social media sites that exude immorality and open cursing. Then, they take what they've learned at home to school and continue in a vicious cycle of parents teaching their children, siblings teaching one another, children teaching other children the cursing, condescending words and attittudes, haughty behaviors, violent outbursts, and much, much more. Much of the bad behavior is underwritten by inattentiveness and unrelenting anger created in the home life of the child as the parent(s) are either minutely aware or completely unaware of the influence of their pervasive out of control personalities upon their own children. The following depictions of stories and anecdotes have been dramaticaly changed to protect the privacy of every individual.

Children see and hear:
1) Parents arguing with one another with name calling, condescension, growling tones, and possibly cursing.
2) Parents' belief systems as they make racial epithets about people who are different than they are.
3) Illicit gossip against other people at home, in the barbershop, or stylist's chair.
4) Illicit gossip against other people as they get into the car after leaving a church service.
5) Mean-spirited expressions emanating from a lack of self-control, personal anger, and the overwhelming sense of unhappiness as they blame their spouse, their children, the school, or other system, for their own problems.
6) Parents committing acts of betrayal against their mates and their friends and not caring, or, thinking through that their children are learning how to do what they do.
7) Reckless domestic violence in the home where they learn that violence is a viable form of communicating.
8) Their parents lack of love and attentiveness through alienation, alcohol and drug addiction, sex addictions with boyfriends, or girlfriends, addictions to pornography, and an overall withdrawal from a normal family life because, "I ain't feelin' this no more, I want to go do what I want to do."
9) Their parents lack of self-discipline when the parents refuse to discipline the children because they don't know how, don't believe in it, or simply do not care. The lack of discipline in the home accounts for too many extravagant urges that go unpunished leaving the child thinking, "I can do anything I want and nobody can stop me." This includes a child as young as one and a half to two years of age when they're at the playground, church, daycare, or school and

they want to test the limits of their possessions by biting and hitting other two-year old's that want to play with the daycare toys. Children must have discipline until it's time to leave the nest for good.

10) The abdication of the responsibility to discipline effectively in the parents' minds is a current cultural phenomena where a parent will have a completely rebellious child, and yet, will place all of the discipline responsibility onto the daycare or school, then, vicariously, or deliberately, placing blame on the institution for any errant behavior.

One major observation I have made regards the open cursing that is so prevalent in the school systems, playgrounds, and gymnasiums these days. Cursing is not a sign of intelligence as so many folk are being led to believe these days, it is actually a sign of the lack of self-control, as well as self-discipline. The lack of self-control is one of the main culprits at the bottom of the majority of bullying comments/behaviors made towards others. Other parents, who have children in schools, corroborate this social change that not only pervades the school systems, but is in open harmony with the media culture. I spoke with a teacher about the openness of cursing at her school and she said, "Yea, they call each other names like that until somebody is in a bad mood, then, it isn't funny anymore."

One late afternoon, I was sitting on a park bench listening to one of my coworkers who was being made to mediate between the boys and the girls with all of their shenanigans that they were doing to one another, or just being offended by one another. This coworker was one of the best mediators I've have ever observed. She was a mediator par excellence.

All of a sudden, one of the kids came up to me and said, "Mark cussed a girl. He just told Karen that she's a b----."

"Where is Mark?" I asked.

"I don't know, he was over there."

"Go find him and tell him to come to me."

The boy finds Mark and sends him to me. Mark arrived directly in front of me, turned to his side and looked down and away.

"Mark, did you call Karen a name?" I asked.

"No," he said.

"Have you talked to Karen?"

"No."

"Are you telling me the truth?"

"Yes."

Just then, five other children showed up, including Karen. They stood around to listen and participate in this inquisition.

"Did you call Karen a curse word?"

He shook his head "no".

Four of the five children were shaking their heads "no", as in, "That's not right!" One boy came over to me and said, "I'll tell you what he said."

I said, "OK, but only tell me the letter. Do not say the word..."

He lunged towards my ear, and whispered loudly, "He called her a b----!"

I looked at Karen and asked her, "Karen, did Mark call you that name?"

"I didn't hear Mark say anything to me," she shyly whispered.

Her girlfriend beside her said, "Oh, that's not right, he did call her that!"

Mark continued to stand there in front of me, staring at the ground.

"OK, I want all of you, except for Mark to go out there and play on the playground," I commanded.

"Mark, sit down here beside me."

Mark wearily sat down beside me and I asked him again, "Did you say that word to Karen?"

"Yes," he responded.

"Do you know that's a bad word? Why would you call her that? You do know that it's a bad word, don't you?"

Mark simply looked down and did not answer. I felt confusion around him. I asked him again, "Do you know that that word is a bad word to call a person?"

"No," he said.

"Why are you so angry, then?"

"I'm not angry," he said.

"Well, people sometimes use words like that when they're angry with someone. You're not angry with her?"

"No. She's my friend. That's how we talk."

Here, I had to take pause. I did not expect him to say that.

I asked, "Who have you heard use that word?"

"My mom."

"So, that word is spoken in your house?"

"Yes."

"How often?"

"Every day, that's what she calls her friends and people on the phone."

"Well, what I want you to do is to stop calling anyone that name, it's not a good word to use against someone, OK?"

"OK."

"I also want you to apologize, to say you're sorry, to Karen and to the others around so that they know that you apologized. But let's make something clear here. Just because you say that you're sorry, it doesn't mean anything if you go back and do it again. The sorry I'm talking about is repentance. It's saying that you'll not do it again. Just saying you're sorry is not enough. You have to stop using that word. OK?'

With his head still held towards the ground, he said, "OK."

"Now, get up and go apologize."

While he was gone, I realized his confusion. I was saying that that word is a bad word, and, yet, his mother uses that word every day in the household. Essentially, I was calling his mother "bad" and didn't realize it.

He apologized and in less than three minutes, he was sitting back beside me on the bench expecting a more severe punishment. We talked a bit more and then I set him out to go play with other children on the playground.

The "b" word is a terrible word to call a female. It is not cool, or kind, it's despicable. Stop calling the females in your life that word!

Cursing is not cool. It demonstrates a lower standard of communicating that reveals the heart's desire to remonstrate on such an immature level that the user is otherwise unable to verbalize.

Parents do things and say things in their own homes and, oftentimes, have no idea what they're doing to their own children. I heard from a retired fourth grade teacher that the worst experience of her 30 year teaching career involved a little fourth grade girl, who, in her most rebellious state, cursed the teacher to her face as loud as she could in front of the entire class with every curse word known to man, repeatedly, and would not shut up. She said that she took the girl by the collar and walked her down the hallway to the principal's office and said, "Here, you can have her!" The teacher went home so upset and told her husband that she had never, in her life, been talked to like that little girl did that day.

She soon retired.

A teacher told me about one of her students, whose name is Vince, who had been set to sit in the class over by himself. Vince was fidgety, always getting up, moving around. He didn't do anything bad, as in disrespectful or rebellious, yet, the whole day he was socially disruptive. He had his own personal bottle for water in his possession that, he said, needed filling. The bottle was translucent, so you really couldn't tell what was in the bottle. During the day, he was accustomed to filling his own water bottle up at least three times a day and he was constantly requesting to go to the rest room.

He would talk to himself, talk out loud, and cause others to be inattentive. The teacher was constantly saying something to him and he would do what she said, then, go do something else. At the end of school one day, they were all in conversation waiting on the bus. Vince, flipping his personal water bottle around in his lap asked her, "Ms. Smith. have you ever had Red Bull Peach?"

She replied, "No, I've never had that particular drink, I've heard they have a lot of caffeine and a lot of sugar. Why do you ask?"

"My mom puts one in my water bottle in the morning. It's sweet!"

She smiled at Vince, wryly, realizing that this child who has been set aside in the class by himself, has private tutoring in math, is always getting up like he's on speed, or a sugar high, is being given a beverage that is high in caffeine (at least 80 grams), taurine, a natural stimulant and 27 grams of sugar.

I do not know if it is happening each morning, or, if it is possibly in lieu of his breakfast. What I do know is that his own mom is giving it to him, not thinking through what the consequences might be or the effects that it would have on him and on his class.

Have you ever heard the phrase from the Mom to the son, after the Dad has left again, "Son, your Dad has left us again, that makes you the man of the house"? I've heard children say such things about having been given parental expectations as young as five years old.

Do you think that a young boy understands what that means, "You're the man of the house"? What is that expectation, or, perceived expectation doing in the mind of that child? Marital separation and divorce places untold stress onto children that the parents either do not know, or, do not care about. Unfortunately, divorce is so wickedly prevalent in our society that the children become collateral damage and the expectation gets repeated often, "They're resilient, they'll get through it." That is a lie from hell.

In his confusion, this same five-year-old boy will find himself expressing himself in no uncertain terms by getting up into the other children's space, on the playground, or, in the classroom, invading the space of the other children in attempts to lord over the children in a bizarre kind of authority displacement.

Giving a five-year-old the responsibility of being the man of the house is quite daunting, even if the Mother did not mean for the phrase to be taken seriously. How is the son supposed to know that if something is said by the Mother, or the Father, that it was only said in jest, or in despair? It is role distortion to the child. The child is a child and in no way can he assume the role of the adult. It is an impossible task for the child. The child is going to struggle with this Mom-given authority and power, which, in reality, doesn't exist, but he does not know that. He doesn't know what it means to an adult, to be the man of the house. He can only sense what it means in his five-year-old mind and the consequences of this expectation will lie covered in the child's unconscious until it gets acted out in attempting to rule, or parent others, not knowing why he's doing it. Parental separation and divorce are bad enough on the child's emotional state. It is far too much to presume adult responsibilities on a child who is incapable of understanding or fulfilling that role.

Not only do children learn role distortions in the home as a result of marital separation, divorce, and gender manipulation, they also learn from the lack of attention that the parent(s) refuse to give to the child because the parent is so wrapped up in themselves in social media, that, in like manner, they give their child social media experiences as young as two years old.

Social media, for a child in the home, is a substitute for real relationships. The child learns from the parents that if the parents are going to be on their phone talking, facetiming, face booking, facing whatever, that that particular instrument that the parent is holding in their hands is more important than the child is. It's called "time given". Parents will give more time to social media than their own flesh and blood. Here is where the substitute comes in and supposedly baby sits and takes care of the child. It used to be the TV, or the radio, now the child has been given a phone, and in that phone, or tablet, are their friends, their movies, their stars, their pets, and their substitutes for real life. In social media, no one is guarding the hearts and minds of the child. Parents have been duped by social media twice over here, once, by spending enormous amounts of time there themselves, and second, by offering their child up to the gods of whoever for whatever is most convenient at the time. What are our children being taught today? It would seem to me that morals, ethics, the simple matters of right and wrong and the ability to learn self-control are being left unattended at the behest of the beast of social media and the parents are responsible for what goes into the minds of their own children. Then, they send their offspring off to school full of what the world has to offer with an attention span of sixty seconds, or less.

Perhaps one thing worse than a poorly managed adult is the absence of an adult which creates opportunity for the children to teach their siblings and their friends others things that a mature, loving adult would caution against. An example is where learning to curse comes into play. I learned to curse from my friends down the street and similar words were periodically heard coming from my parents and brothers and sisters. For example, today's usage of the word b---- is so prevalent, one might believe that there were no negative connotations to the word. The word's literal meaning is a female dog, slanged into a belligerent, or hostile woman, has transmogrified and is now used as an endearment of affection among women and friends and, at times, is connected with the word, "beautiful". A student walked into a class and exclaimed, "Hello, my beautiful b-----." After interviewing the student as to why she did so, she told me, "That's what we do, that's what we call our friends." She said she learned to curse on the playground in the second grade by the older fourth graders.

It seems that in our culture today, many of the definitions of words have been manipulated, or, downright changed to suit the culture because the culture demands what it wants when it wants it and anything goes as long as "I" get my way. Children repeat what they hear on the playground, as well as, what their parents say and do. If the parent is out of control, then it makes sense that the child would follow suit.

By the time some children have gotten to middle school, their out of control behavior exhibits itself in presumed authority over other children, or students. I have observed a particular phenomena in the classroom where the bossiest kid, whom I call the class police person, is actually the one who is the most out of control by yelling throughout the classroom the commands that an irritated teacher might propel, "Shut-up, Be Quiet, Do what I say, etc." and then, they go on talking to their friends as though they are exonerated from obedience to doing what is right. Perhaps, they learned this type of behavior at home from a parent who would yell at them to do a particular thing that they, themselves, were unwilling to do. It is called hypocrisy and the other children wince at the hypocrites who do not see, or hear, their own misdoings. They could have also learned it from another student who believed he could command his territory, when, in essence, the classroom is not his territory, but, in his mind, it is.

Years ago, I had the opportunity to be around a group of juvenile boys, living in a group home for the wayward, drug addicted, rebellious, and all-round bad boy crowd. We were about to eat dinner together and then one of the guys began describing what most people would call 'Sloppy Joe's' as he started out by saying, "Yea, we *could be having*...." But what he was describing wasn't exactly what was in Sloppy Joe's.

One of the other boys called him out on it and said, "That's not what's in Sloppy Joe's!"

He replied, "It is, if you're in prison!"

Someone asked, "How do you know?"

He responded sheepishly, "My Dad's in prison."

The room was silent.

Then, another boy said, "My Mom's in prison."

Another said, "My Dad just got outta jail."

Then, another spoke, "My granddad's in prison."

I responded, "Charley, your granddad's in prison?"

"Yes."

"Why?" I asked.

"For abusing my Mom all her life. My Mom's been to jail."

"For what?"

"For trying to kill my granddad."

Little Bullies Can Become Big Jerks

During this spontaneous confession time, many of the boys confessed that one, or both parents had been in jail, or prison, at any given time. For me, it clearly explained, not excused, but explained, their behavior when I had seen them at their worst. And, then again, some of the boys could have been "keepin' up with the Joneses'" with their espousing something to be tough, but it wasn't exactly true.

When parents, or supposedly, responsible adults, act in particular unbecoming ways, even if they' re not aware they're doing it, no person in their lives is immune to their destructiveness, especially the people closest to them. We will reap what we have sown and, in turn, ridiculously sow what we reap in vengeful means to protect ourselves from others who may be worse than we are, or have been in our past. The fields of pain that we have sown, in some, we have seen, and yet, still others we will not see until a time it is brought to us under conviction and its terror terrorizes us to shame that only our God can release us from. Under conviction, He shows us who we are and who we have been, not to terrorize us, but to bring us under conviction of His Holy Spirit, to restore us and to bring about change in our lives.

At another church, a young girl was crying relentlessly. I got some tissues and sat down with her. I was quiet while she cried. At the right time, I asked her what was going on. This was her response:

"Sheila told everybody that my Dad just got out of jail."

"Is that true?"

"Yes."

"How does she know that?"

"She found out from reading my journal. I don't want people knowing that about my Dad."

"How did she get your journal?"

"Sammie stole it from my desk and gave it to Joey. He read it and let Sheila read it, too. Then, she told everybody in class what was in it."

"Where is the journal now?"

"My teacher has it now."

I sat with her until his tears subsided and became her friend, if only for a moment.

I tell this story for the evident. Little children doing something simple in taking the personal story of a classmate and distributing it at will and mocking their classmate in the process is the epitome of ignorance in bullying and shaming another person. Even still, I cringe in empathic humiliation for the child. My heart cries for her, and, yet, in her humiliation, she is experiencing the collateral damage of a Dad who has had quite a bit of misfortune and is trying to get his life back on track.

One of the ways to a child's heart is to say their name with love and care. I've tried to remember children's and youth's names and to attach a note of affection, or endearment with their names. If you think within yourself, you will take note of those people who not only remember your name, but remember you because they care for you and you know they care each time they say your name. I've had teenagers to run up to me and say, "Say my name, Mr. Lursen, say my name!" because they had heard me say their name as one who cared about them as a person, and not as a number. The opposite is also true, if all we can do is say a child's name with disdain and anger, they'll remember that and be the lesser for it.

This writer isn't the only person who cares for the children of our land, there are populations of principals, teachers, counselors, and youth ministers. Parents, though, are the ones who are ultimately responsible for the loving care of their own children. We all need to change and stop the bullying so that our children are not sacrificed at the altars of our own selfishness. It is past time for us all to care for every child we come in contact with.

Throughout the years, I have sought change in my own life. I try help others, but I do not seek to change them, because true change takes place in the inward parts of every person. A person can change. A person has to recognize their proclivities, their own personal sinful ways, take issue with these ways, and then learn to rehearse in their mind how to avoid the pitfalls before them, and change their responses to certain situations. A student who, in the past, had constantly stayed in trouble at school because of his personal anger issues, was helped by a counselor to recgonize his own emotions, particularly anger. He practiced recognizing what made him angry, the feelings involved, and when he would become angry, he could say, "I'm angry, now what...I need to redirect, refocus, replace, or change my location..." as opposed to lashing out in rebellion or violence. He received a miracle.

The desire to change is in many people, but the ways and means to change are left somewhere else in the atmosphere, oftentimes leaving many people with accepting their pitiful, ugly natures and relegating themselves to act like a child and say, "Well, that's just who I am and I'm kinda proud of it...I didn't mean to do it...I did thus, and so, to that person and it was funny, it was revenge for what they did, or simply put, they got in my way, and they got what they deserved."

May God have mercy; may Christ have mercy and grace for our ways that, as parents, we have treated our children in our pilgrimage through this life. May we learn what a real jerk is, confess our despicable ways and learn to change so that we can bring light, life, restoration and peace to others that we come across in our future walk through life.

Chapter Two

The Early Formation of a Jerk
A Mini-Autobiography

"Bad dogs aren't born, they're maaade..."
from "Night at the Roxbury"

Real jerks aren't born that way; they get lots of training at early ages from parents, siblings, extended family and worst of all... daycare. I'm 62 years old and, yes, a very long time ago, I went to daycare. At the daycare, I vividly remember sitting in front of a black and white TV watching the news and the events covering the President John F. Kennedy assassination. That's how old I am. I also remember one of the childcare workers when I was younger, and, I have to laugh at the word, childcare, as an oxymoron. There were children, but caring for the children was not the top priority. I guess it was what my parents could afford and, I, in turn, put my children in some very precarious places.

In any case, at this daycare, there was this female worker that, to me as a five-year old, looked like she weighed over 200 pounds. She was the punisher of the group. She punished the little children at her discretion. She literally used her full weight, at times, to sit on an errant child, typically a boy, if the child would not shut up, or had done anything that warranted a punishment. I remember the anticipation, the screaming and the choking suffocation of the child to "give in" to the weight of the woman sitting on the child.

It seemed that in watching these punishments, that I would choke on my own breath as they suffocated momentarily and then, to release and suffering in squeamish cries as she would rock them to sleep from the experience. I learned to fear, not only there, but the thought of going there. Anxiety became me. I learned to cooperate and obey for the fear of the punishment far outweighed the thoughts of doing anything outside of perfection.

One afternoon, when I looked through a doorway into another room, I saw my younger sister, who was under two at the time, scampering on all fours on the floor underneath a line of baby cribs. The childcare workers were chasing her with belts to give her a spanking for whatever it was that she had done. I remembered them flinging their belts at her as they knelt to try to grab her. I feared, so I turned away from the doorway. Then, as expected, I could hear her screams as she was beaten with a few belts and then put down in a crib to take her afternoon nap.

I remembered having to pee a lot as a child. I would wet the bed and often, my Mother would check the bed at night, as it would be soaked from my own sweat from me having pulled the covers over myself so that I could hide and not come out until morning.

I recall being in bed at night and listening to my parents argue unmercifully with each other. My Mother would constantly accuse my Dad of flirting with other women. They talked a lot about sex in the household. Indirectly, sex was a daily topic of conversation, as was contemptuousness, railing, jealousy and adultery.

By the time I was five years old, I had already learned to be selectively mute. My Mother would be angry with my Dad after more accusations and then repeatedly tell me, "You better learn to take care of yourself, 'cause by the time you get a little older, I'm leavin' this house, 'cause we're gettin' a divorce!"

My parents eventually divorced when I was around 30 years

old. By that time, I still felt like I loved my Mother in a very reserved and cautious kind of way. My Dad moved on and married another woman that made our lives even more difficult and complex for decades.

As a result of my personality and the culture of the home in my formative years, I learned to play alone. As long as I could play outside, in the sandbox, with my army men, and later, the GI Joe's, I was very comfortable. I played outside all day long by myself. I had to be called in for meals. I learned to read and read and read; it seems that that has always been my safe space. Possibly it was there that I learned that I was OK with myself, but I had no idea, as a child, that what was being deposited into me was being stored deep within. The tone and disposition of the home was all that I knew of what a home life was. It did not occur to me that other families did not treat each other the way we were treated and in return, treated one another. Alone, I could control my world. When I was around others, I submitted and tried to do as I was told. That included my peers, as well as, adults. By the time I was seven, I had learned to listen, obey and keep my mouth shut.

That's a little bit of how I grew up at home. One very wonderful thing happened when I was six, or seven, years old. I was given my first puppy dog. I loved dogs and named him Tiger. I still love dogs. There have been only a few years of my life that I have not had a dog, or two. Tiger was how I spent my days. I would stay outside with him and sleep on his belly and he on mine every chance we got. Our next-door neighbor had a son, who we'll call Sammie. Sammie was a year, or two older than me. He and my older sister, Teresa, whom I loved, would pick on me and hit me like a punching bag. I think that they always wanted me to hit back. They would tell me to hit back, but I could not muster enough gumption and inward strength to raise my arms and protect myself. I can remember Teresa trying her best to get me to fight back, but I wouldn't. I couldn't. I did not know that I was a non-violent person, but I was, nonetheless.

One afternoon, Sammie and I were playing outside in our backyard and he started his bullying again. I had this residing anger in me, but I wouldn't defend myself and he knew it. Tiger was there and was always watching it all. This time, Sammie hit me and knocked me to the ground. I had had enough. In the moment, I could see the fear on Sammie's face. I shouted to Tiger, "Sic' 'em". Tiger did. Simultaneously, Sammie turned to run and Tiger lunged at his hands. Sammie ran and Tiger snipped at his hands all the way to the edge of our property. I called Tiger off of him and back to me. I was not alone for Tiger was with me. I smiled and rubbed him and told him how good a boy he was.

The next day, Tiger was nowhere to be found. Nobody said anything to me about it. I don't remember even asking my Mother. I kept his disappearance to myself. Inside, I guess I figured that either my parents, or Sammie's parents had "taken care" of my Tiger. I remember not playing with Sammie anymore after that day. They soon moved away and I was glad. I learned that people should move away if they can't treat people right. I also learned that the thing I loved most could, and would be taken away from me at any time, without warning. I had to act right and be good and placed Tiger deep down inside of me in silent rage.

The home that I grew up in had two sides to it, as I think many homes do. There was this extremely friendly, vivacious side that we all presented well at church and at school. High school is where most of our family excelled. Both of my half brothers played football and both had become president of their classes. They, along with my older sister, Teresa, all won most popular in their respective graduating classes. I alternated being class leaders with a good friend, Alan. I had won other awards and my overly glorified self-esteem soared with the support of the high school teachers and church leaders. I was a very proud young man and looked forward to a life in church ministry as I could sing a little bit and began moving forward in music ministry.

That other side, though, was still at home. I believe that by the time I had entered high school, I had developed a muted inner rage from my home life. My parents hardly ever got along. My older, half-brother, Bill, was murdered in Vietnam by his own men over drugs. I grew up in a pornographic household where Playboy magazines were purchased and left out on the counter and in closets where I had access. My view of women was kept secret, locked up in my mind and body. Women had become objects of desire, to be lusted after. We do not have to go far in wondering why there is so much sexual harassment and abuse as young boys, and now, just about everyone though internet pornography, is taught that the human body is to be treated with promiscuity, and lust. I do not believe that bad boys are born, they are made at home in the arguments of their parents, hypocrisy, little, or no moral teaching, the neglect of mature supervision, the inattentiveness of loveless marriages, mean-spirited neighbors and in the lack of personal human responsibility that we are personally accountable for our behavior. A child does not know that, but if they see adults who refuse to be responsible, they think that is how life is.

There was no accolade large enough to satisfy my Mother. I was in the running to win some quality award in the state of South Carolina in my sophomore year in high school that had to do with my personality and my intelligence. Hence, she used that possibility as an opportunity for me to graduate early, because I was smart enough to do so, to boot me out of the house, and then go to the local technical school to learn a trade. I think she wanted me to become a plumber. I wasn't 'feelin' that idea, as I was growing in my popularity at school, playing football and other sports, and learning that I could sing. My life became a living hell at home, as a result, and whatever rage I had, I took it out on the guys on the football field. On the football field, I could hit well. I was extremely focused and my inner rage was in a controlled environment. No one, that I was aware of, knew what I was going through. That made me happy. I learned to live two lives…one with the inner well-kept rage at home and one of the most popular at school. At school, I was friendly, honest, and courteous; at home, I was at the mercy of the mood of my parents and my personal life of duality.

Some days were good, of course, otherwise, I could be easily challenged on my memories whether they be true, or false. My Mother was one of the most giving, generous person's I've ever known. She loved to bake cakes and the more extravagant the cake, the better. Coconut was her and my favorite, until she learned the indulgence of the almond joy cake, which was chocolate cake, having each of the three layers smothered in gooey fudge and coconut, topped with almonds. My Mother always kept Christmas well. One year, when I was in middle school, my Mother made the decision that we were to receive no gifts and that a needy family was coming over to eat and receive Christmas from all of us. The needy family had a father with no job and a mother confined to a wheelchair. There were four children who had Christmas that year and a weeping mother in a wheelchair that I will never forget.

Later in years, I recall taking my Dad out for lunch and I needed two dollars in cash to finish paying the server a great tip. He was having a spell of dementia, off and on, yet, he was attempting to comply with my request. He pulled out his wallet, opened it up and showed me all of the cash that was there asking me again what I was wanting. Comically, he thumbed through a stack of one hundred dollar bills, looking for a couple of one dollar bills. He had one, one dollar bill and at least fifteen to eighteen one hundred dollar bills. I paid with a debit card.

I believe that my Mother was a wee bit disquieted in her spirit. She was, for the most part, unhappy and unfulfilled. I think my Dad was, too. I do not know why they could not get along. I remember my sister Teresa telling me that when our parents had gotten a divorce and my Dad had found another woman, that he was smiling and tremendously happy. She recalled that she couldn't remember the last time that she had seen him smile. My Mom and Dad needed counseling, they needed outside help, but did not seek it. I discovered much later in life that there had been an adversarial family member working her work in between the two of them all along.

Even now, it seems sometimes that I wish a wish upon a star that I could have waved a magic wand over the two of them so that their first love for each other would have been regained. I regret not having a magic wand for the love and the happiness lost in them.

It was during the times at home that I learned how to manage this dual personality by my opportunities. However, as I progressed through life, my inner stresses, fears, anxieties, and turmoil were never dealt with appropriately, so that the old inner rage would come out in my tone of voice that made me sound like the jerk that I had become. I recently learned from my Aunt that the "tone" was from my father's side, it was how they grew up in Iowa. Now, it was in me and my family was hearing and feeling the brunt of it. I was a brewing pot of anxiety, fear and fear of failure, so, if perchance, someone would happen to get in my way, they would get directed with a tone in my voice to scare a bear. By the time I was in my thirties, the private dual life had come to ripeness in spiritual failure. I became a current day prodigal son not knowing which way was up. I was the biggest and worst jerk that I knew, yet had no idea on how bad I was, nor how deeply the effects were that I had on other peoples' lives.

I had a seminary degree, was in the ministry, but left the ministry and withdrew into work, having started a janitorial cleaning service. I stayed to myself. I realized that, at the time, I felt like I did not have the grace for pastoral ministry. For the most part, in my cleaning business, I kept my head in a toilet, cleaning toilet after toilet. I learned to never say "no" to whatever someone wanted me to clean. I felt dirty and so I cleaned up after people. I decided that my penance for my life's sin would be found inside of someone else's toilet.

At the time, I did not know that we do not get to choose the arena of our penance.

I prayed, wondered, meditated and pondered at how I had lived this life that was supposed to be all things Christian, but wasn't. I doubted my existence in faith, as I should had, as well as, my own personal existence. I did not know why I did the things that I did. I did not know what drove me to do the things that I did, the things that I said and how I lived my life. I once told a group of churchgoers in a meeting one night that if I could reach down into my throat and pull up and cast out the tone of voice that I had grown up with, I would do it. But, I couldn't.

Professor J. Gresham Machen had this to say regarding the effects of personal sin, *"The truly penitent man longs to wipe out the effects of sin, not merely to forget sin. But who can wipe out the effects of sin? Others are suffering because of our past sins; and we cannot attain any real peace until we suffer in their stead. We long to go back into the tangle of our life, and make right the things that are wrong – at least to suffer where we have caused others to suffer. And something like that Christ did for us when He died instead of us on a cross; He atoned for our sins.*

The sorrow for sins committed against one's fellowmen does indeed remain in the Christian's heart. And he will seek by every means that is within his power to repair the damage that he has done. But atonement at least has been made – made as truly as if the sinner himself had suffered with and for those whom he has wronged. And the sinner himself, by a mystery of grace, becomes right with God. All sin at bottom is a sin against God. "Against thee, thee only have I sinned" is the cry of a true penitent. How terrible is the sin against God! Who can recall the wasted moments and years? Gone they are, never to return; gone the little allotted span of life; gone the little day in which a man must work. Who can measure the irrevocable guilt of a wasted life? Yet even for such guilt, God has provided a fountain of cleansing in the blood of Christ. God has clothed us with Christ's righteousness as with a garment; in Christ we stand spotless before the judgment throne." (Christianity & Liberalism, page 110).

I am still, obviously, researching these things, but, if you're still with me, you can see the threads of input in my early years that got worked in and worked out throughout the rest of my life. At this point, though, let's make one thing perfectly clear...although my parents were who they were, I do not place any blame on them for my terrible decisions and behavior. They had the most influence in my life, indeed, but I do not blame them for my life. The responsibility of me lies squarely with me, and no one else.

**A friend playfully told me that I am the
"Jerk Whisperer", the "Jerk Decoder"
I know too well their tendencies and am able to connect
the dots of the very best and the very worst of jerks.**

We learn to be jerks and unashamedly accept the behaviors of our pitiful lives because of the clouds of witnesses that have gone before us. We live to be like our teachers, our parents, our peers, our preachers and our politicians. We learn to be friendly when it suits us, or benefits us, and then we take what we think we deserve. It is this dual personality of hypocrisy, a wicked selfishness of self-preservation that drives many a person to jerkism because, as the world teaches, it is more pleasurable to take...it is more self-aggrandizing to give others their due, whether they deserve it, or not. Thus, the life of the royal jerk, unfortunately, lives on in many of us, vicariously, perpetuated in our own behaviors that, either, we refuse to change, or simply do not know how to change.

Mister or Madam, it will not suffice when, in the end, you come before God and say, "Well, I loved my dog and he knew who I really was. I was not that bad. I'm a good person. They made me who I was. It was their fault, my parents, my brothers, my neighbors." No. He will be looking at you and holding you accountable for what you have done. You are responsible for what you have done and said, and what you became. This is all about you and you alone. I pray that you decide to read on for the second half of this book details some very specific ways to acknowledge what we have become and ways to change our thought patterns and our behavior so that we do not continue to ride a lonely horse down the road of discontent finding ourselves alone at the end of a dark-end road.

Chapter 3

What Exactly is a Jerk?

"You will know them by their fruit..." --- Jesus

Imagine that you are in an office building, on the first floor and you proceed to the elevator. You push the button to go up to the tenth floor of a fifteen-story building. When the elevator doors open, there is already a gentleman in the elevator who, as you enter, you smile, but he gruffly sighs and wiggles his right eyebrow as if to say, "Get in the elevator already and push your g----- button!" He parked in the parking garage at ground level and the atmosphere, aura, or ever how you want to put it, in the elevator is in control by this very communicative, non-speaking person. His demeanor is annoyed just because you're there, breathing his air. You feel as though you are impeding him somehow, because when you pushed the button for the tenth floor, the fifteenth floor had already been lit. You quietly move to his left so that he is not breathing down your neck. You hear him breathing and you think to stop breathing a moment so as to not interfere with his air.

As the elevator goes up, the bell rings and the elevator halts at the third floor. He gruffles. Another person that you know gets on to go up to the eighth floor because that's where her office is; she smiles at you because she's all cheerful and such and quickly surmises that all of the air in the elevator has evaporated. She stops smiling at his rejection of joyful humanity. She sheepishly, yet quickly, pushes her button. He sighs loudly, breathing openly through his nose passages in a huff. As the door proceeds to begin its close, another person is heard beyond sight and exclaims, "Please hold the door!"

Your friend reaches for the open-door button. The man behind you gruffly pushes through lightly shoving your shoulder and hers and defiantly closes the elevator with the needful person left standing there with two heavy cases of files in her hands. The elevator door closes. You can hear and feel the tension in the small elevator room. All you can sense is his gruff breathing and you can't wait to get to your floor, knowing that in the future, if you ever see him again, you'll smile, but take a pass riding with him again.

Jerks are easily annoyed at petty things when their sense of control is impeded. They will take over when given the chance.

You are sitting in your boss' office. He has lied...again. This time, it is affecting your reputation among your peers because he is accusing you of abusing the company car and talking about you behind your back. You have asked to meet and you confront him about the car policy. He disagrees with your assessment and clearly written policy, yet the only reason he is annoyed is because it's you. You ask him about his lying about this event as well as other instances of him not telling the truth. His response is, "I know that I was not entirely honest with you in the beginning, or with the board, but I needed a job. I'm here now and I'm the boss. If you don't like it, leave. Now, get out of my office!"

Jerks are disrespectful. They will lie in order to take advantage of a situation, or another person. For the most part, they simply do not care who they hurt, or the damage they cause to another's reputation or efforts. To some, the jerk sees others as losers and he/she is above that crowd.

Your spouse arrives home from work as you can hear the squeals of the tires rounding the curves in the street and into the driveway. The car door slams. The front door opens and slams. Your son runs to greet his Dad and Dad is oblivious to his son and brushes him aside. He doesn't say "Hello". He doesn't say anything. He is in his mood...again. He stammers off to the bathroom. Your son, and his son, as well, goes back to the television and stares blindly into it and you can see the hurt and rejection leaving his face as it is replaced by a sternness of reserved emptiness.

Jerks have little self-control. When their world is out of their control, they lucidly take it out on the ones closest to them, hurting others, disregarding the pain and eventual loss that they will inflict.

These are just a few of the instances where a jerk has entered into someone else's space and because of the need for their control to be asserted, they blatantly exonerate themselves from their actions as they inflict their personas onto others.

We know a jerk when we see one in action. We know them by their fruit, their words, their tone, their demeanor, and their behavior.

Many years ago, I was working in a restaurant chain as an assistant manager. I had not been doing the work for long, yet had moved to a store that needed my "expert" expertise. I was being my typical jerky self that day, barking out orders and commanding the scene like the general that I thought I was. The kitchen manager was back in the kitchen and I was manning the front line. He said something to me through the kitchen window and I said something back to him. He and I were not in any kind of friendly relationship. He didn't like me and I didn't care, I was his boss. He said something derogatory and disrespectful and in the middle of a lunch rush, I said, "I want to see you back in the office, NOW!!" I wasn't going to put up with this type of disrespectful behavior any longer. He was going to change. I marched back to the office in the back of the store and he followed me. When I arrived in the very small, closed off office that had one door, he was behind me holding a 9" butcher knife up to my nose. I took one step back. That was all there was left of the room. I was not afraid as he waved the knife to my chin because in my mind, I figured if he was going to use it on me, he would have shoved it in my back as we walked back to the office. I do have to say, though, I respected what that knife could do.

As he waved his knife before me, he told me that I was to never, ever tell him what to do again, or he would kill me. I stood my ground, unshakable, and agreed with him. Inside, I knew that I would never tell him what to do again, because I knew he would be fired. He was fired later that afternoon. I can honestly admit that my tone of voice and personal disposition drove that relationship to where it went. In the moment, I was oblivious to my demeanor, and did not care. I have since learned to care.

Birds of a feather really do flock together. Jerks flock together in teams, in ownership, and at leadership levels. They feed off of people who are hired to do their bidding, or who simply work as volunteers, and for the most part, are unaware of their propensities until repetition of jerk-like behaviors and dispositions become recognized. If a jerk acts the fool to another jerk, he will get a jerk's reward. Newton's third law of motion states, "For every action (force) in nature, there is an equal and opposite reaction." A jerk will be a jerk because that is his nature. He may acquiesce when confronted by a more demonstrative force for he is generally not stupid...not all of the time, anyway. He will recklessly ruin relationships because of his thinking that he is somebody significantly more important than others. He does not care about others' input, their opinions, or their feelings unless there is some ulterior motive to allow someone else to be themselves around him/her. To the jerk, his plan must be exercised and any other idea better fall in line with his plan.

Chapter 4

Dealing with the Imperative

"People will do what they are allowed to get away with."
Dr. Ben Carson in regards to the pervasive disrespect of authority and attacking police officers with impunity in the New York City boroughs.

Dr. Les Carter, a renown psychotherapist, has written a few books, 29 books that I know of. One that has impressed me is, *"***Imperative People: Those Who Must be in Control***"*. Dr. Carter admits his own imperativeness and his growth in it and through it. He describes an imperative person as not a personality type, but a thinking type. Imperativeness is an attitude that crosses all personality types in this respect – the need to control.[2] Imperative people have the need to be correct, get solutions, stick to the script, or the plan, at all costs and that includes ruining relationships along the way. Dr. Carter teaches that right thinking includes genuine concern which trumps being correct and that the influential life is proved in its effectiveness in others.[3]

Some of the negative traits of the imperative person in their keeping of control are: shouting or cursing to coerce cooperation, presenting a false sense of superiority, being picky, petty, and critical, and attempting to manipulate how and what a person should think and act in order to adhere to proper guidelines.[4] All of this causes others to feel angry, build defensive walls and become paralyzed in knowing how to react. [5]

This is where I have learned to try and stay away from my own "imperative NOW". That is, expecting another person to see things my way or to do certain things the way I expect them done. I am not talking about restaurant branding or the corporate world here. Here, I'm just talking about living and me attempting to make, or coerce someone else to fulfill my standards and personal choices. When I insist that a person do it to the tee, exactly my way, I'm being ridiculously imperative as well as being a lousy jerk. I have had to learn to listen and to listen well to others. It takes work to not be selfish. It takes acknowledgment to know my propensities and to stop acting out when someone doesn't live up to my expectations.

At times, the standards, or expectations, are not unreasonable, it is my insistence of them and the way I come off, mean-spirited, ugly tone and beady eyes. We have to look at ourselves in the mirror and listen to ourselves in the way we communicate with others.

Dr. Carter also says that the need to be dominant supersedes all other concerns, "...control can also come through silence, quietly or directly being uncooperative, it doesn't listen or pretends not to hear what you say..." [6]

Through much of our being imperative, or a jerk, there is this inability to recognize that we are responsible for our actions. There is a corollary here, too, that there is an inability to recognize that we are not in control of other people's actions. It is the superfluous self that believes he/she can and does control others. We may influence, but we are not in control of them.

There is also this desire to force change on other people. This is evidenced in road rage when one party is justified in expecting another to obey the rules yet they want to become the enforcer and all rage breaks loose in a driver's mind when the other driver doesn't do what is expected, lawful, or otherwise demanded by the offended driver. The driver's steering wheel becomes the power substance to many a jerk insisting that their pathway be protected at all costs.

Stephanie Moulton Sarkis, PhD, a licensed and board-certified counselor, as well as, the author of **Gaslighting: Recognize Manipulative and Emotionally Abused People – And Break Free,** wrote a piece in Psychology Today, "Six Reasons Why You're a Jerk". She lists six reasons and here is a portion of what she had to say:

1) You only talk about yourself – Yes, you may have climbed the Himalayas...swam the Amazon...or any other enviable accomplishment. That doesn't mean everyone wants to hear about it *ad nauseum.* Be interested in other people.

2) You tell offensive jokes/use offensive language – If people aren't laughing, or they're doing a polite "tee hee", your joke was not funny. If your whole point was to make people feel uncomfortable...you have succeeded, but you look like a jerk...if this isn't a joke you'd tell your grandmother, don't say it.

3) You're pushy and intrusive – Don't ask people why they haven't had children yet, or when they're going to lose their baby weight...or, their past mistakes.

4) You're mean – People don't like people who are nasty to others. You may tell yourself *I don't care if people like me.* Wrong. You do care when you get passed over for promotions because you're the guy with the chip on his shoulder.

5) You show disrespect for others and their opinions – This doesn't mean you have to agree with someone. But even if their viewpoint is vastly different from yours, they should still be spoken to with respect.

6) You whine and/or complain – Bringing up concerns and whining/complaining are different things. Bringing up a concern means that you are actively seeking a solution to said concern. Whining/complaining is just stating something you don't like just for the sake of stating it. [7]

While I was in college, I went to summer school for a couple of months to make up a few classes. There was one dorm for men and one dorm for women. I was a resident assistant in the men's dorm. We had a resident director, my direct supervisor, who owned a moped, a mini motor cycle; he didn't drive a car, but I did. At night, he would put his moped in the dorm hallway so that it wouldn't get stolen. In my mind, I figured that if he wasn't going to use his marked "Resident Director" parking space, then, I would. He was given a parking sticker for his specific parking space that I was unaware of. Hence, I started using his space because I had a car. It was convenient for me and it made me all the more special because I could park my car in "my" guaranteed spot at the door. One morning, I went to my car and there was a parking ticket on the car window. I'm thinking, "This is not right, I'll go to the college security and talk them out of this..."

I went to the security office and asked to speak to the Captain. When I walked back to his office, he did not get up and welcome me. That was a sign that I did not recognize.

He asked, in his slow Southern accent, "What can I do for you, Mr. Lursen?"

I smiled, thinking, "I'm gonna get out of this..."

I explained my predicament, that the RD did not have a car, but had a moped. I had a car and I simply didn't see any reason why I shouldn't be able to use his parking space, being that it wasn't being used. The Captain listened to my 'sob' story, as I was quite animated not wanting to pay a $25 fine. That was in 1980, and in 1980, $25 was a lot of money to a college student. It still is, by the way.

The Captain listened attentively to me and then he had this to say, "Mr. Lursen, when my deputy took that mind-readin' course, he failed it. You can pay your $25 fine at the door. Have a good day."

He moved slightly in his swivel chair motioning his hand towards the door as he spoke.

In that moment, I realized that I was never in control of this situation. Chagrined, I got up from my chair, did something weird with my mouth in a pout and as I passed through the door, he said, "Close the door behind you." I did. I paid my fine, and did not park where I wasn't supposed to park again.

I began to learn, in a very small way, that, like the deputy, I could not read another person's mind, nor could I change another person's mind, no matter how I sweet-talked or tried to sell him on my goodness, or my ignorance. Attempting to change someone else's mind, or attempting to change another person's behavior is about control...manipulative control. It is an inward self-deception of arrogance and pride.

If you have been married for a good length of time, you will have already discovered that you cannot change another person. Change comes from within. The desire to be that new, or better person is there...in the within. Many do not know how to crack open that person in the within, because the desire to be in control is so insatiable. Some people will do just about anything to think that they have ultimate control over themselves by attempting to control their circumstances, others, things, other peoples' things and, all the while, have very little self-control within themselves.

Dave Ramsay, the financial expert, has stated many times that the worst abuser in the household will have absolute control over all of the money. Household money control oftentimes develops into grave attempts of spousal control, directly and indirectly. Larry Burkett, who has passed away, was the creator of Christian Financial Concepts. He used to say that the majority of all arguments in the home and the leading cause of divorce was over money.

Control also comes in the form of isolation. Dr. Phil and others attest that isolation is the foremost weapon for the abuser through isolating their victim from family, finances, and eventual emotional and mental health.

Perhaps the best training field for the jerk mentality is seen every week on television sets. All ages of folk watch collegiate and professional sports. Not all sports participants are jerks, but it doesn't take long in the duration of any game, to see behaviors of dominance, violent outbursts, and uncontrolled rage. Little children watch all of this rage on TV and society makes it "cool" to be a jerk. The winning desire of any team is to control the line of scrimmage, to control the box, to control the paint, to control the ball; to control the opposing player.

Control is elevated in our society in all forms of social media. All of human nature is driven to achieve control and maintain it regardless of the costs or consequences. The idea of control gets preached in the airways, the pulpit, the politician's stand and wherever a perceived leader can emerge to say, "I want you to be empowered! You are somebody. Nobody can tell you what to do. You are empowered with "whatever" from on high…don't let anybody get in your way!" I once told a hyping preacher that "empowered ignorance is dangerous". We are seeing the results of empowered ignorance today in our nation. Empowered ignorance is shouting to people, regardless of their education, experience, or abilities, that they can take what they want, take it all, go get yours, get yours now, take control, you're in charge...and on and on preachers, politicians, and leadershp gurus falsely empower people to grab somebody else's stuff and call it their own, or simply take control of other people's lives and do to them whatever you wish because you are now empowered to do so.

"If any man desires to come after me, let him deny himself. For what will a man give in exchange for his soul, the whole world? He who loses his life for my sake will find it, but he who keeps his life, will lose what he thought he had." --- Jesus

A person's thoughts about a particular belief come first, then, the belief becomes substantiated in further meditative thoughts regarding the belief. For example, if you receive the idea that you are gifted to give good advice because you believe that you gave good advice to someone and then, to someone else, the repetition seems to substantiate the belief that you have it within yourself to give another person good advice. If you take this belief and start acting out on it by giving practically everyone advice on how they should live their lives, whether they asked for it, or not, you might find that you are the only one that thinks you give good advice and everybody else shuns telling you anything else about themselves because they have discovered that you are basically a nosey, busybody that has nothing better to do than to share your personal prideful wisdom with the world, whether it be wrong, right, or, sought after. I learned a long time ago, that if a man wants to know what you think, or, if he needs your help, he'll ask for it. Otherwise, remain silent, wait with patience for the right opportunity when the person in need comes to you and seeks your help.

The movie, "Tulip Fever," was about the 17th century tulip bulb explosion in Amsterdam, an explosion of prices to magnificent proportions. All sorts of folk were buying tulip bulbs at exorbitant prices because public mania over a flower had grown to even more extavagant absurdity. Brokers were trading tulip bulbs like they do stocks and commodities on the New York stock exchange today. One of my favorite lines from that movie was this: when a nun was giving the truth of a matter to one of the main characters, she said, "We cannot say we know more than we can know, leave the rest to God, He doesn't like mopers."

This, I believe, is a partial reflection of the philosophical rationale in Immanuel Kant's, *"Critique of Pure Reason"* (1787) in that we can know what we know...beyond that, we should remain silent.

Perhaps, this is why the incompetent, the haughty, the proud, and the jerk justify themselves before their superiors, in experience and intellect, with their suggestions on how things ought to be done their way. They speak to hear themselves speak, knowing little to nothing of which they speak, and they, being the incompetent, do not realize their incompetence because of their own, undying and unreserved incompetence. Speak about what you know, beyond that remain silent. Those that portray the manner that they speak for God, whether they think they be apostle, prophet, pastor, or preacher, speak much about what men have said through time about God and what they think, yet speak very little about what God might have actually already said in the matter. There are those men and women of God who lay at the feet of Jesus and honestly desire to know Him in holiness, yet there are others where incompetence reigns in place of spiritual authority as a result of vanity and salesmanship, as well as, the lack of spiritual relationship to the risen Christ. A lie is a lie and ignorance abounds when the people of God do not recognize a sheep from a goat, or a wolf from a real servant of God.

How does your presence with another affect that person?
Are they made glad that you are there with them?
Or, are they regretful that they ever knew you?

A New York Post article, entitled, "Brain Scans Reveal How Badly Emotional Abuse Damages Kids," discusses how the brain scans of emotionally abused children reveal stark differences from the brains scans of normal children who have not been victimized emotionally, physically, or through neglect. The study found that emotional trauma and eventual suffering contributed to developmental delays, memory problems, stress, and life-long complications. (New York Post, Brain Scans Reveal How badly Emotional Abuse Damages Kids, Andrea Downey, November 2, 2017).

I have known many and diverse groups of people. I have known many people that I have loved and needed in my life. I have also known people that were destructive to me as I have been to some. At the time, I was sorry to have been with them as they contributed to my loss of jobs, contracts, or opportunities. However, some time later, I could see where they helped me to become a better person, or helped reveal things inside of me that needed to be eradicated. The mirror image of my dark imperfections in some people bespeaks the truth beyond comprehension…when I see my darkness in others' disposition, voice and behavior, corrective inward change is the needful result in me. And still, there have been others that if I had never met them in my life, it would have been quite all right with me.

Chapter 5

Confessions to a Jerk

Through many years of pastoral counseling and serving in various types of ministry, I have encountered countless numbers of people who have been battered, betrayed, used and abused by other people. Confessions abound of wrongdoings, however, with quite a few people, there were some extraordinarily similar types of abuses abounding in most sectors of life. I have asked some of these people to reveal some of their thoughts as it relates to this subject matter.

As you read through their responses, please remember that I asked the responders the following three questions: What do you believe are the characteristic traits of a jerk? Can a jerk change? And, I asked them to write out a "Dear Jerk" letter to that special someone(s) in their lives that presented themselves as a real jerk that left an impact in their lives. The impact that the jerk leaves behind is the point here. I did not ask them if they felt like a victim, or, if they felt that they had contributed in any way to the way they were treated. Some people think that people get what they deserve. I don't. Some people think that it takes two to create turmoil in each other's lives. Maybe, maybe not, it depends on the circumstances. Relationships are complex. There isn't always a villain and a victim, nor is there always only one person at fault.

I changed the names of the contributors to protect their privacy. This expose' is a reflection of some of their thoughts in presenting varied perspectives, yet very similar in emotion to the three questions asked...

Stephanie writes, "the character traits of a real jerk have to include: Selfishness, always having to be right, never admitting wrong-doing; and justification beyond belief. These jerks I have encountered have no idea they are jerks-- they are not doing this on purpose-- it is sort of inherent in them. They think everyone else has the problem and that they have no issues.
Dear Jerk--

I am convinced that you will have no idea about what I am speaking of. Please know, that I pray for you. I have forgiven you for this reason—I believe that you did not know any better.

Forgive me for putting you on a pedestal. If I had not done that, you would not have fallen so far in my eyes. I went in with the eyes of a naive innocent child-- everything was sunshine and rainbows. That is not your fault.

It is my responsibility to at least give you an opportunity to gain sight--to no longer be blind to your actions. The first hurts came from the revelation of lies you were telling about your own life. That is when I first discovered that I was an enabler. I was not even aware of that, but in my desire to save our relationship, I began to protect your lies and cover you from anyone who could have offered you help.

Then came your abuse of boundaries that I felt were understood in any marriage. Of course, it all became my fault, but I was still treading water, holding in my arms--our relationship above the water.

In the final stages, you could no longer hide your disdain and disgust for me; hating me for every good thing that I seemed to represent that reminded you of every wrong thing that you were doing or saying.

When the dust settled, all that was left was remnants of what used to a family. Broken children that will take many years to mend, and forever all broken people. Sleepless nights and endless questions of, 'Did I do enough to salvage the unsalvageable?'

I must thank you, though, I would not be the person I am today if you had not been a jerk. You have not only hurt me, but our children as well. I do not thank you for that. God bless you.

Do you believe that a jerk can change? Only by the true saving grace of Jesus Christ. There is NOTHING anyone else can do or say to change them. The jerk must recognize that he/she needs help and cry out to Jesus-- and it will be then and only then that there may be healing."

Jeremiah writes, "The traits of a real jerk are self-centeredness, have no empathy; they are inconsiderate and presumptuous. They are divided people, split within the self. From this inward brokenness, they attack others. They break and splinter people, leaving their victims with the inability to put their splintered lives together once again. You can't put a piece of wood back together after it has been splintered and so the difficulty begins with the people that they leave behind. I believe that a jerk can change, however, in order to change, jerks need to have an accountability partner, like a mentor, in order to walk through their behavioral transformation. They need the Shalom of God, the real peace of Jesus Christ, and not the substitute of religion that so many turn to.

Dear Jerk, I write you in a place of exhaustion due to your self-absorbed behavior. I have been stripped, broken and bruised at the hands of your egomaniacal persona. I have been sacrificed at the altar of your selfishness. You have left an open wound and a trail of blood behind your narcissistic pursuit of manipulating the masses. Your reign is now over in my life due to the understanding that your deep fear of others seeing you as weak, frail and vulnerable has now come to the forefront. Know that you are now exposed to the truth of your weakness and that you no longer have any power over me."

Jim says, "The characteristics of a real jerk are found in their behavior. Pure selfishness. That has to be the top one. Most of the jerks that I have dealt with, and even when I am being one myself, have had the self in mind first and foremost. Another characteristic would be rudeness. Have you ever met a kind jerk? The perfect jerk only thinks of himself, what he/she wants right then. They don't care who's insulted for them to obtain their goal(s). Can a jerk change, of course they can. Being a jerk is not a permanent disability. My jerkiness, along with most of the jerks I come in contact with, is not their only personality trait. One way I have changed from being a jerk is by stopping and listening to myself. Asking if my actions are the best way to get what I want. Maturity and wisdom also play a part.

Dear Jerk, Why? Why did you call and share our private conversation, even after I asked you not to? Is it that you think that my wishes aren't valid? Did you think you were helping, or is it that you just know more about it than me? Your actions have me really upset. It seems that me asking you to not call the tile installer didn't work and you called him anyway. All because of what reason exactly? Is it because you are selfish? Maybe it's because you don't trust me to handle the situation. When are you going to let me do my job and not interfere? Let me explain something to you, I don't need you to always swoop in and save me. I am more than capable of handling sub-contractors, especially with the jobs that I am supervising."

Samatha had this to say about the jerks in her life:

1) A person who only thinks of himself. He has no idea of what he says to someone that can change that person forever. (Ex. You could lose some weight. You will not make it in the real world.)

2) Has no patience. They are constantly rushing around with no regard for others. No time for politeness.

3) Feels the world owes them something. Always rude and demanding, then when he's given something, he feels it was not enough.

4) Feels no remorse. This is the worst criminal behavior. They can hurt someone and not feel any remorse, or shame. A jerk can mark a person for life. They can destroy an innocent person's dream. They can make people feel they are not worthy. An example of this is abused women. Unfortunately, some stay in a relationship because they are so beaten down. It's also when a parent who can show no affection for their children. This can lead to a child to grow up with extreme insecurity. They can hurt someone's feelings and it seems to not bother them at all."

Larry writes...a jerk is an annoyingly stupid, or foolish person; an unlikeable person: one who is cruel, rude, or small-minded. To me, a jerk is:

1) Guarded - protected – They only engage in generalities in order to avoid accountability. They are unwilling to change because they don't think they have to. They manage expectations by trying to limit their failures...and keeping control and attempting to control their own destiny. They don't let anyone in; they are indifferent by not taking a position and evading responsibilities. This makes it easy to blame others for their decisions, mistakes and failures.

2) Fearful – Fearful of losing, of being hurt, of disappointment, of not having power, of being wrong, of not being

needed, and of not being valued.

3) Lack trust – They are unforgiving for they keep score of wrongs against them, real or perceived. They carry pain; they lash out, verbally, or through actions as punishments. In their minds, no one is as good as they are; they are perfect and no one can do what they do as well as they can.

4) Insecure – The jerk is threatened by roles; they seek credit for what they did not accomplish, while discounting others for their contributions. They are willing to listen to what they classify as an "expert" or someone they personally qualify as "qualified" and all others are beneath them. They are not happy with who they are, with their looks or their status. They refuse to see or admit their own flaws. They pride themselves as independent, but this is because connecting with others would require too much work and, in their minds, that doesn't add perceived value to their day; it threatens the system that they've created.

5) Selfish – A jerk is rooted in selfishness. They pride themselves on calling this "independence". Why? This is a learned behavior from someone, something, or some series of events that were detrimental to one's healthy growth relationally. Being a jerk is a defense mechanism in order to go through life as pain free, as possible, from relationships, all the while, unintentionally causing a wake of pain and destruction in their path. They have a, "I'm gonna get you before you get me," mindset.

6) Blame shifting – Some people are raised in a culture that promotes a false perfection. This can lead to creating a life that can mask their imperfections while making others feel guilty about their own imperfections. A jerk can wreck havoc, becoming an emotional terrorist, if you will,

on anyone that is not aware of their propensities. They accomplish this through manipulation, control and blaming others. The pain that this type of person leaves behind is gruesome and unhealthy for in their combative nature, they create a sense of depression, causing others to lose their sense of self-worth. In their most personal of relationships, trust is abused and lost. Perhaps the most destructive aspect is this…if they perform their traits in front of and with children, they spawn, or clone, more jerks.

7) Unwilling to change – Without work, a jerk is incapable of change. Everyone can change, that's the power of free will. However, without serious intervention, or a major life event, a jerk won't be willing to change. Even then, the will to be a jerk will have to be overcome on a moment, by moment, basis. Without the recognition and agreement that the sum of a thing is greater than the part of the thing, there will be no need for the jerk to change. I've seen organized religion as a breeding ground for jerks; not only does it birth jerks, it trains them up in the art, ensuring to keep them in bondage. Only when a jerk is humbled by the loneliness and destruction surrounding them, will they begin to see the need to change. It is my belief that only the Holy Spirit can bring an individual to this place of right relationship with God and with others."

Regarding a realty experience, Linda had this to say…

"The main character traits of the person we encountered were selfishness, self-centeredness, arrogance, and ignorance. These are evident when the person smooth talks the suspect into believing that he is on their side. You do not realize it in the beginning, but you eventually find out that his interests were first and foremost. Because of his arrogance, he becomes ignorant of what is actually the best outcome for both parties. This realtor had no idea the value of our home, the desirability of the location, or our history with the neighbors. Had he known all that, and listened to us, he would have potentially made more commission when the home sold by listing it at the price we suggested. As it happened, he lost the sale completely by not doing his due diligence in helping us to find another home to purchase first. They lost the commission on our purchase of another home. Everything was done at their convenience. In the process, we experienced a slight financial loss, emotional turmoil and distress (I had a full blown panic attack over signing the final contract), embarrassment at pulling our home off the market a week after it went up for sale, disappointing prospective buyers, and breach of trust. If the realtors had listened to us, it would have benefited them and us as a family, but they simply didn't want to be inconvenienced.

Can a jerk change? Yes. We believe a jerk can change, but it will take an event of great magnitude to cause change, usually one that would result in great loss or alter a core value held, because surely even a jerk has at least one core value."

Shelby's experiences with jerks have led her to see that a real jerk is someone who is selfish, doesn't think about others and doesn't care about how their words/actions affect other people. Jerks lack compassion and lack a desire to understand and care for others, especially when others are different from themselves. I've worked with and been in community with plenty of jerks that make the lives of those around them unpleasant. They have a reputation for being mean, hurtful, arrogant and selfish. Most of the jerks I've met are either lacking self-awareness and don't realize they are a jerk. It could be that they simply don't care. A jerk can only change with a change of heart. Being a jerk is a heart issue."

Another had this to say, "Jerks are selfish, prideful and have an inability or an impaired ability to care for someone else other than themselves. They lack a relationship with Jesus who exudes love and caring. They exist in their own world that revolves around them. They cannot see an issue or needs from someone else's perspective. They may have been damaged or scared in their life and therefore take out their anger and frustration on other people. They may also be people who feel entitled.

I believe a jerk can change. I've seen young people who bully, change as they mature, and experience punishment for their actions. I've also seen jerks change when they go through a life altering experience or hardship that helps them see what it feels like to be hurting. I watched a friend of mine change his selfish ways and soften as he cared for his sister with cancer. There needs to be a "burning platform" that forces them to shift their thinking. I also believe God allows satan to inflict pain to get people to change. He is the great Gardener who prunes us. Some don't change until it gets very serious and others have epiphanies along the way that cause them to change their ways. If you believe in miracles, then you have to believe that if God wants to reach someone He can. Our God is a God of restoration and forgiveness for those willing to turn from their evil ways and repent and turn to Him (ex., thief on the cross, Paul's persecution of Christians, etc). It is the miracle that happens when you finally submit your life to Jesus. It requires a person to choose God, submit to God and be obedient.

Dear Jerk, for twenty-eight years you have lorded over others and held your position of power. You try to pretend you care about people. You put on an extreme act. Behind closed doors you lie and slander others. You violate the values of trust and respect and "doing the right thing" continuously even though you hold others to this high standard.

Little Bullies Can Become Big Jerks

I worked very hard and productively for you for 22 years and you know that I was instrumental in growing the company you lord over by several hundred million dollars. You always said it was not necessary for people to lead the company from Dallas, that you wanted strong leaders all over our offices. You changed the game on this promise and lured me there with the promise of the CEO role. You changed your mind and decided not to give up your position of power as soon as I arrived in the moving truck in Dallas. You didn't have the courtesy to be real with me and forced me to make you admit you had changed the game.

During the time in Dallas, my mother-in-law committed suicide back home in Virginia. We were not there with her to see more closely the demons of anxiety and depression she was dealing with. None of us had a chance to say goodbye. I happened to be in town the day the event occurred. I had to wipe her blood off the floor. It was beyond terrible.

Your love of money, pride in your position and your dishonesty did serious damage to my family. My daughter has the day she committed suicide tattooed on her ribs. You dangled a carrot, asked me to move my family, and then you were dishonest about what you were doing. You almost ruined us emotionally.

Through it all, it was incredibly challenging and humbling. Thankfully, God promises us that He can use ALL things for good for those who are called according to His Purpose.

We were able to see things very clearly and reprioritize our lives and refocus on what is best for our family by looking at things from God's perspective (Thanks to you, Terry Lursen).

We have made new friends, started a new company, written a book about the struggles (to help others), stopped drinking and even helped a man avoid committing suicide.

All praise honor and glory be to God who walked with us

through this terrible valley, helped us climb up the mountain again and learn from our experiences. Our family is stronger and closer for having survived this experience and we pray we can be used to help others going forward.

I have forgiven you for what you did, and I pray for you frequently. I pray for God to reach you somehow and perform a miracle. You need a change in heart. I pray that God will use me as He sees fit in this process. "

Monica had this to say... "I know this is probably not completely what you wanted when you asked me to respond, but it is what I lived with. I know that many counselors and advisors think that having the victim write a letter helps, but it really doesn't. It just makes you realize that you cannot stop someone from doing something no matter how bad it is but I had learned that a long time ago. I didn't have the extreme physical abuse that many have which is one reason that I didn't understand how abusive he really was. It was mostly mental and emotional until the last few years. That is what confused me so. As I have told others, back when we were young, only physical abuse was a reason to leave someone and I thought I was strong enough mentally to fight back when he got angry. I got better at seeing it coming so it could be forestalled which I hear all victims do, but it is like a growth that gets bigger and bigger until it eats up everything. It just destroyed the person who was so full of life and fun.

Coping with the destruction at my age is rough because it comes down to reality of life and what you want to put up with to have your needs met. I can't afford to not have this job, yet I would dearly love to have my old life back before he began cheating. I truly believe that is what turned him into the monster he finally became full time. I have been told that bi-polar people continue to worsen as they age and that he would have done this whether he cheated or not. There is no way to know. It is what it is and I have to live with it. Thank you for letting me at least try to make sense of this but I still know no reason for such destruction. However, the Good Lord has been looking out for me with my job and many friends to support me, so I will just keep keeping on.

I believe that I lived with a person with a split personality. There were days, weeks, months, and even years when he was the nicest person. In the beginning, he was dependable, honest, kind; he seemed to be bi-polar with anxiety attacks, but was not the bad guy until I came to know this other person. The bad guy even took on a different look in manner including how he stood. The nice guy had a humble walk and stance, but the bad guy threw his shoulders back and walked with extreme confidence. He was haughty, arrogant, and disdainful. When the bad guy showed up, he was often drinking hard liquor and showing off. But the next day, he was so embarrassed, and I began to realize that he didn't remember things. There were times when he would be appalled at how someone else acted and really couldn't believe how much of jerk that person was. It took me a long time to see that he really didn't see himself doing the same things. In the early days and having young children, it wasn't hard to keep hard liquor away. I didn't notice his bad behavior as much with beer, and since neither of us like cheap wine, wine wasn't a problem. But time, money, and resentment with peers began to overrule the nice guy. By the time he reached the bad guy all the time, almost 30 years had gone by. He couldn't hold the bad guy away at that point.

When he was the bad guy, the following is what he acted like. Sometimes I was so embarrassed at his behavior and if I said something, I got the "you are such a goody two shoes" or "wuss" or something similar mocking me. As the children aged, they called him out too and he would act all coy and laugh at their boldness and act like it was funny. But you could tell that it made him mad. They didn't know it, but he took it out on me later. The good guy never did these things, so it reached the point of not really knowing which one you had. He worked hard to put on the show for his parents, my mother and family, and co-workers but even they all began to see him changing.

 Then, as his behavior got more erratic, he began to not trust himself, so he got quieter and more resentful. His anger got much worse after he betrayed himself by cheating. His behavior became more bizarre. At some point in his mind, he decided that he deserved to cheat on our marriage and it was, of course, my fault.

 It was always someone's fault that he didn't get want he wanted and that is the pattern that I noticed getting worse and more often. It had to repeat enough for me to see that every promotion, job reward, etc. that he didn't get was someone else's fault. After he left our home and our divorce was final, he was acting out around his coworkers. She was very much in the picture the last 5 years of our marriage and he married her two years ago. However, he was still acting bitter around people, blaming me for the fact that they didn't like him anymore even before he married her. He showed his true colors to his coworkers when he resented a young admin getting work that he didn't. This was a year after our divorce, so I was completely out of the picture. You see, nothing had gone as he had planned so his anger of everything was out in the open.

 Now that his blow up is over and he is in a happy place again, he is back to acting like the nicest guy again; showing off as the life of the party and coming across as very happy. He has left all his past behind him and no longer working with the old company, so the stress is gone for now. The pattern repeats, though, and it won't be long before he resents that he doesn't have what he had or wanted all along. He will get bored again and then the anger will be back. That pattern got faster and faster as the years went by.

What would puzzle me so is that after the coworker or boss was not a direct influence on him, the good person would become a great person again. He would talk about them with the most detached type of voice as if he had absolutely no animosity against them at all. My son has said that he has talked about me raising the kids beautifully as if I did it all by myself. I have heard that before and it is bizarre because it is so detached from reality. Or, maybe that is where the mind truly is which is a scary thing.

I know that this is more than you want but it is hard to describe the bad guy and not let you know that he wasn't always like this. I certainly would have left him years ago if he had been. The jerk was a person who, in the beginning, came out sometimes out of the blue and would go back in for long periods of time. But he took over every time he felt that his bosses were against him. I have no idea how much of a smoldering persona he projected at work, but we got the bad guy at home when that happened until that boss moved on or he did.

I was the last boss that was in his way. He was already in a depression over his mother's death (his mother was his first boss) when the old girlfriend persuaded him that only she loved him and knew him better than his own family. So, I gather that in his mind that even though she dumped him many years ago, someone else made her do it and, in his mind, I was the interloper. I really have no idea because his mouth had a whole series of lies about why he wanted to be free. It was so totally bogus, that the judge and the lawyers, including his own lawyers, were astounded. I was afraid that the judge would think he was not sane, so I took him to mediation instead of having him talk on the courtroom stand. He had already shown his bizarre logic at the financial hearing making the judge angry. My lawyers were afraid that if he spoke on the stand anymore, I might not have gotten free.

Dear Jerk, I feel so sorry for you because none of this had to happen. You were given every opportunity to be the good guy that you could be. That was a happy person who was trusted, but you refused to do that. Your family begged you to get help for your anger and you chose the person who was feeding you the lies you wanted to hear. You chose someone who did not know you and only had her selfishness driving the lies that you fell for. You not only threw out our love, but everything you helped to build…our emotional, and financial past and our future with our children and grandchildren to be. None of this was in your best interest. Your reputation is now gone, shattered to family and coworkers. But what is really so bad is that your children can never trust you again. They will endeavor to try hoping that the good person will come back, but since you aren't really happy with yourself you will destroy that, too.

You had a conscience that you betrayed and that is what will destroy you. You are now just playing a game and pretending to be happy in front of others, but the lies you told and the one you are living will destroy you. This is especially the liar that you are living with and in time, your paranoia about her will creep into your mind and destroy it. She lied to you initiating this and lied to her family, too, just as you did to yourself and your family. You lost everything you had which was more than enough for anyone. You had a loving family, great job, wonderful friends, and coworkers who supported you. While there were some who saw your true colors, most did not and now they have lost all faith in you. Maybe this is your true self and the nice guy was the fake. If that is true, it makes it even sadder."

Little Bullies Can Become Big Jerks

Marie had this to say, "The character traits of the jerks I've experienced can be any number of: insensitivity, condescending, rude, inconsiderate, malicious, selfish, mean, manipulative, deceptive, dishonest, evil, unaccountable, unhappy or dissatisfied, insecure, unbalanced, unwise, dramatic, emotionally unintelligent, and/or bitter.

The wounds they create in others can be frustration, heartache, loss of time, and a loss of money. If I had my chance to tell that person, I would tell him this...

Your discontentment in life displaying itself in mean and undeserved, ungodly behavior is weak and ugly and a waste of the blessing we have all been given called life. A real man looks like Jesus, not Lucifer, and does not let anything hold him back from being the best version of himself.

A jerk can change if that person has an awakening to their true heart and behavior as wrong and decides to get help, deny him/her self, and do the right thing, whatever the cost. Humility and reverence followed by submission to Christ and an outward expression of love where negativity previously lived is vital. The Holy Spirit is the most efficient way to change. It takes action immediately and consistently to break a pattern of behavior and intentionality to act in a loving manor in lieu of the negative behavior previously deemed as "jerk behavior" to now bare fruits of good, the Holy Spirit: Galatians 5:22-23 - love, joy, peace, patience, kindness, goodness, faithfulness, gentleness and self-control.

The following traits are of the devil and most commonly display themselves in a "Jerk" manner: "the acts of the flesh are obvious: sexual immorality, impurity and debauchery; idolatry and witchcraft; hatred, discord, jealousy, fits of rage, selfish ambition, dissensions, factions and envy; drunkenness, orgies, and the like. I warn you, as I did before, that those who live like this will not inherit the kingdom of God."

Further connection to "jerk" like behavior lies at home or is manifested in many of the spirits below: There are always underlying issues when someone is deemed a "jerk". Commonly it is a weak self-defense mechanism for those with feelings of inadequacy, abandonment, poor self-esteem, abuse, etc. If those issues remain unaddressed then healing and correction are not possible and the devil will be all the more content for that individual to stay in a mean and negative state disconnected to his purpose and ineffective till he exists no more.

The Bible has many names for evil spirits: Deaf and dumb spirit (Mark 9:17-29), Evil spirit (Luke 7:21; Acts 19:12-13), Familiar spirit (I Samuel 28:7), Foul spirit (Mark 9:25), Lying spirit (II Chronicles 18:20-22), Perverse spirit (Isaiah 19:14; Romans 1:17-32), Seducing spirit (I Timothy 4:1), Spirit of an unclean devil (Luke 4:33), Spirit of antichrist (I John 4:3), Spirit of bondage (Romans 8:15), Spirit of death (I Corinthians 10:10, 15:26), Spirit of divination (Acts 16:16), Spirit of error (I John 4:6), Spirit of fear (II Timothy 1:7), Spirit of haughtiness (Proverbs 16:18-19), Spirit of heaviness (Isaiah 61:3), Spirit of infirmity (Luke 13:11-13), Spirit of jealousy (Genesis 4:5-8; Numbers 5:14), Spirit of slumber (Isaiah 29:10, Romans 11:8), Spirit of the world (I Corinthians 2:12), Spirit of whoredoms (Hosea 4:12, 5:4), Unclean spirit (Mark 6:7; Luke 11:24-26)."

(When a person doesn't tell the truth and he/she leads you down a road to where you actually invest a portion of your life in time, energy, and planning for the future and you do all of this with a heart full of love and hope, the total investment becomes dashed and tainted. Deception is cruel, however, dishonesty in a committed relationship costs the person left with empty hands more than the deceiver can attest to understand. Real, Godly love is not blind.

Real Godly love doesn't go looking for trouble in the dark places of another, but it also doesn't expect to be lied to.)

A good friend had this to say, "I believe some of the characteristics of the jerks I have known are that they are insensitive, short-sighted and caustic. They laugh at others expense, often unaware of how bad a person they really are. One of the consequences is that people develop a lack of tolerance for the Jerk. They will refuse to cooperate with that person; will spend far too much time discussing how bad that person is with others, which causes one to take on a "negative" versus positive view of that person.

I haven't hung around long enough to see a real jerk transform into a better human being. I normally give several chances and when I've had enough, I stop interacting with them.

Dear Jerk, thank you for showing me, in the clearest forms possible, exactly how to NOT manage the efforts of others. It has been an eye-opening experience to watch you jockey for a leadership role you were too immature, irresponsible and unqualified to perform effectively. I learned from you that being "aggressive", "bullying", "domineering", "egotistical" and "short-sighted" are attributes I would never want to align myself with, as you did. From a close distance, I watched you run a once thriving, profitable, well-respected company into the ground. I watched you alienate, demean, belittle and bark at some of the most talented people I've ever had the pleasure of working with and it was sad to watch them run for the hills rather than work another day with you.

As professional women in the workplace, it is never required that we take on the attributes of men in order to be heard, understood or respected. You seemed to have missed that class and found cursing, hollering and shouting at good people, to be more effective. The end result was that rather than stirring up inspiration, motivation and excellence, you killed all joy, annihilated any passion for the work, and wound up with a bunch of people who simply stopped giving a damn.

Thank you for confirming for me that compassion, fairness, honesty and integrity are still admirable qualities worth embodying; and that while you possess none of those today, there is still hope that they might reign down, slap you in the face and rest squarely upon your heart one day."

Chapter 6

The Very Worst of Traits

The very worst of traits that any person can have is this:

"I do not care about other people. I do not care about you. I care about what I care about. I do not care if you live, or die; are hungry, or filled. I do not care if you are poor. I do not care if you do not have a place to live. I do not care if you do not have a job or cannot provide for yourself and your family. I do not care if I step on you while you're down, or in my way...I simply do not care for you. I do not care what you have to say, nor do I care about how you feel today. I only care for me."

A prideful person's perspective is particularly personal.

If while you are reading this and you are compelled to dwell on someone else that you know is like this, please stop, because you are already on the wrong road. I am very certain that all of us know others who may have this lack of caring in their lives, but what have you done to prove that these personal traits are not yours? Be honest with yourself first and always.

Jesus had this to say to people who are this way in their hearts:

"When the Son of Man comes in His glory, and all the angels-with Him, He will sit on His glorious throne. All the nations will be gathered before Him, and He will separate the people one from another, as a shepherd separates the sheep from the goats. He will place the sheep on His right and the goats on His left.

Then the King will say to those on His right, 'Come, you who are blessed by my Father, inherit the kingdom prepared for you from the foundation of the world. For I was hungry and you gave Me something to eat, I was thirsty and you gave Me something to drink, I was a stranger and you took Me in, I was naked and you clothed Me, I was sick and you looked after Me, I was in prison and you visited Me.'

Then the righteous will answer Him, 'Lord, when did we see You hungry and feed You, or thirsty and give You something to drink? When did we see You a stranger and take You in, or naked and clothe You? When did we see You sick or in prison and visit You?'

And the King will reply, 'Truly I tell you, whatever you did for one of the least of these brothers of Mine, you did for Me.'

Then He will say to those on His left, 'Depart from Me, you who are cursed, into the eternal fire prepared for the devil and his angels. For I was hungry and you gave Me nothing to eat, I was thirsty and you gave Me nothing to drink, I was a stranger and you did not take Me in, I was naked and you did not clothe Me, I was sick and in prison and you did not visit Me.'

And they too will reply, 'Lord, when did we see You hungry or thirsty or a stranger or naked or sick or in prison, and did not minister to You?'

Then the King will answer, 'Truly I tell you, whatever you did not do for one of the least of these, you did not do for Me.'

And they will go away into eternal punishment, but the righteous into eternal life." (Matthew 25:31-46, Berean Bible)

Chapter 7

The Jerk's Confession

Now that you've gotten this far, and you recognize what a jerk is and you have come to realize that you have been a jerk, or possess jerk-like behaviors, tendencies, and speech, are you ready to confess that you are a jerk? You cannot change what you will not acknowledge. If so, begin here with your admonition and confession:

My name is: _____

I have come to realize that I am a jerk.

I act like a jerk to many people, particularly to the people that are closest to me.

I repent of my being a jerk, or a bully, and exhibiting those behaviors.

I desire to change from being who I have been to others.

I desire to change for my own well-being and for that of my loved ones.

I will to change with the help of God.

I trade contempt for conviction, arrogance for humility, pride for patience, and selfishness for new life in Christ Jesus.

I will to no longer be the jerk of my past, but submit to be the person God has intended me to be for my future.

I ask God, in Christ, for mercy and grace, for His forgiveness.

As He is grace full, so will I be to others.

As He is mercy full, so will I be to others. As He has forgiven me of so much, so will I be forgiving of others. As He has loved me so, so will I to be loving to others.

Your personal notes, date, and signature:

I have been inclined to title this club, "Jerks Anonymous", however, in the real world, although people may not know who the alcoholic might be, everyone and their brother knows who the jerks are. There's nothing anonymous about us.

Chapter 8

How to Stop Being a Jerk

Acknowledge through confession to God – You may not believe in God, but I do and I believe that the only way a person can truly come out from the bondage of selfishness that jerkism provides is to confess it to God. If you've sincerely read through the aforementioned confession, then you've started on the road to doing the right thing.

Admit – Introspection is not enough. Recognize the behaviors – out of the heart, the mouth speaks...out of the hands, the person is. A person will not change what they refuse to acknowledge.

Identify the thoughts, and emotions that drive you to think the way you think and the thoughts that drive you to do the things you do. Identify why you are angry. Start there. Learn to break free from debilitating patterns of behavior.

Understand how your background and human nature contributes to these thoughts and behaviors. Understanding your background does not give you the right to blame others in your past, no matter what they did to you, or to someone that you love.

Recognize that you are responsible for your thoughts, your behaviors. Recognize that your hands are yours and what you choose to do with them is your choice. Recognize that your words are your words and what you choose to say, is always your choice.

Recognize that you are not in control of how others think and that you cannot control others actions. We may have influence, but we are not in control of them. We have to eliminate our own desire to force change on other people – people are who they are regardless of what we think they should be, or become. We can have influence with others, but we should never think we should, or could, control others.

You want to be free to be who you are.
Allow others to be who they are.

I personally believe that I am supposed to be changed from within by the work of the Holy Spirit. The proof of that concept is revealed in my spirit, in my thinking, in my emotions, my heart, then my words, actions and behaviors will follow what's going on inside of me. There must continue to be consistent change from the old person of who I was to the new person of who I am supposed to be.

If there is no change in behavior or words, then it is acceptable to believe there has been no heart change. Let's not fool ourselves in thinking we're something that we're not. The Holy Spirit is holy, therefore what He possesses becomes holy.

The Holy Spirit constrains me to reflect, abide, meditate and change. The change is found in the moments of time. As I mature in Him, my moments become minutes, the minutes, hours, and the hours...days.

"I am changed." I ask the LORD in the power of the Holy Spirit,

'Is there any wicked way in me?" My self-examination and introspection is enjoined to the Holy Spirit's examination and conviction.

Commit your way to STOP doing those things that make you act, look like and sound like a jerk. This is called repentance, where you stop doing the things you've been doing and turn about face and do the right things the right way for the right reasons. If you find yourself doing _____ , stop doing it. If you hear yourself saying _____ , stop saying it.

There has to be a breaking free of consistently bad patterns of behavior.

Confess to those you've injured – This is for those closest to you, your spouse, your children, parents and siblings. This is for that coworker where you have been rudely, or crudely, abrupt or mean-spirited. Apologies are worthless without real change. Biblical confession is first of all repented of. Saying, "I'm sorry", is not repentance. **Repentance is to stop doing the act.** Repentance, then, becomes a part of your confession in that when you go to that family member, friend, or coworker, your lead in is that you have something to confess. You say what you did, what was wrong with what you did and you will work on what you did to not do it again. Do your best to not use words like "never...I'll never do it again..." that only leads to expected failure, because "never" is for eternity. Eternity is beyond our thinking. We can work towards change and, hopefully, not offend again. That is more realistic.

Dr. Les Carter says, in regards to the process of change, "identify – identify your thoughts and emotions...understand (yourself)... your traits of your imperative personality, to control, to be driven by duty, to act superior, yet feel inferior, to be dependent on others' opinions or emotions about you. Be liberated – imperative people can free themselves from the need to always be right...allow yourself to make mistakes...we can enjoy relationships with other people if we are not trying to dominate them." [8]

Will Rogers once said, "Never miss a chance to shut up."

Learn to listen to others with your heart and mind, not just your ears. If you're talking, you're not listening. If you're not listening, you're not learning. If learning about your situation, or about the person you're attempting to communicate with is not important to you, then stop right there and decide to make the other person important.

Elbert Hubbard said, "He who does not understand your silence will not understand your words." Listen to what others say and what they don't say when they're silent.

Listening is one of the greatest gifts we can give to another human being. Emotional and intellectual maturity requires that we listen to others when they speak. Let's be perfectly clear here, though, many of us listen to others just to be able to respond in debate, oftentimes, rudely interrupting.

Don't interrupt people when they talk.

Listen to learn what the other person is saying. Learning to listen is an open door to caring about the person you're listening to. Learn to care about their words, their inflections, their meaning and their means of communication.

**Listen and respect in order
to come to a common consensus.**

Stop making people struggle just to get in a word to your ears. Don't make contemptuous faces or facial mannerisms when others are talking to you. I was actually thrown out of a business meeting one afternoon even though I had not said a word. I was listening with all that was in me, quietly, and, yet, I was responding with contempt for his ideas with my face:

The supervisor said, "Get out of my office!"

"Why?" I responded, "What did I do?"

"I heard what you're saying," he stammered.

"But I didn't say anything," wincing as I spoke.

"It's all over your face. Now, get out of here!" he exclaimed.

Don't make contemptuous facial expressions when others talk.

I have to confess that it is one of my repeated jerk behaviors that I continue to have to work on to avoid doing it. The work is in my mind. If I'm not thinking, "What a dumb idea!" I won't be showing it on my face. Contemptuous and haughty looks come from pride and arrogance, "I can think better", or, "I could do that better", maybe, maybe not. Let the other person share their ideas and thoughts, without your judgment.

Learn to mature emotionally and intellectually. You and I are not the smartest people on the planet reigning high above others with our notions of superiority. Accept that as a fact.

Maturity is a concept of relevance. One can be relatively mature for a teenager, and, yet, the person is still a teenager and is going to act like one in certain instances. In the regard that I am referring to, maturity is that ability to accept responsibility for the self. Immaturity is the absence of serious responsibility:

"Maturity has also been taken into account when determining the fairness of the death penalty in cases involving mentally retarded or underage perpetrators. In Atkins v. Virginia, the U.S. Supreme Court decision banning the execution of mentally retarded persons, was decided on the grounds that "diminished capacities to understand and process mistakes and learn from experience, to engage in logical reasoning, to control impulses, and to understand the reactions of others" was cited as the evidence supporting a reduced view of criminal culpability." [9]

If you take a fair assessment of this ruling, then the flip side to the positive characteristics of maturity would be – the capacity to understand and process mistakes and to be able to learn from experience. You have to be able to recognize when you've made a mistake and be willing to confess it, admit it and repent of it. The immature and irresponsible continue to blame others for their mistakes. They do not learn from their own experiences, but somehow deem others culpable for their wrongdoings.

I was talking with an elderly woman one day and she started making comments about her daughter, who was over 50 years old at the time. The elderly woman clearly spoke in regards to her daughter, "She's immature," as she shook her head back and forth disgusted with what her daughter was doing to her during that time, as well as the actions that the daughter had continued to do over the last thirty years. At the time, I was confused with the woman's statement until I subsequently interviewed the daughter and heard the daughter blame the mother for all of her own mistakes, her own divorces and her own lifestyle. The daughter had been divorced five times by the time she was fifty years old and evidently blamed her mother for the majority of her life choices and decisions.

Also taking from the court ruling we glean that a mature person is able to 'engage in logical reasoning'. It requires a balanced mind and emotional stability to reason with another person in order to simply have a conversation as an adult. We talk, we listen, we listen, we talk. We converse, that takes two, or more people, communicating. We have to listen in order to reason with one another. Habbakuk put it this way, "How can two walk together, unless they are agreed?" The point here is not that we have to agree with what everyone says, but we are required to listen, to reason, to cooperate and come to an agreement, even if it takes much to do so.

The imperative dictator demands the now. When impatience rules an imperative person, harsh words are spoken and cannot be retrieved. If you find yourself getting angry in a conversation with your spouse, slow your emotion, reason with your mind and learn to control your emotions to avoid angry or violent outbursts.

Dr. Harriet Braiker had this to say, "...an overall attitude of mutual respect is mandatory for healthy emotions to develop in relationships. Respect is shown in numerous ways-through what you do as well as what you do not do or say. For example, mutual respect is demonstrated by listening and valuing each other's conversation; by taking pride in the accomplishments of each other and yourselves as a couple...respect is also shown by not using derogatory, patronizing, or otherwise demeaning language toward each other either when alone or with others; by not ignoring or dismissing each other's opinions or ideas; and by not negating or invalidating each other's feelings or reactions." [10]

Controlling our own impulses is probably the most difficult here for the real jerk. The lack of self-control is, perhaps, the jerk's greatest weakness. The lack of self-control looks like this:

1) Mind wandering, including the refusal to control your own thoughts. Not every thought is a good thought, nor is every idea. Take control of your thoughts.

2) If you take control of your thoughts, you'll be better equipped to take control of your heart, the seat of your emotions. An emotionally out of control person is a wreck waiting to happen. Emotionally immature folk scream for attention in words and actions. Emotionally immature folk spend money that isn't theirs and refuse to see, or care, about the consequences of their actions when it comes to spending money or spending frivolous words on hurting people. The emotionally immature person that lacks self-control is loose with their body, loose with their money in overspending, and loose with their thoughts becoming mean-spirited words and actions intended to do harm. Take control of your thoughts and you will take care of your emotions. Stop the angry outbursts. Stop the manipulation of your own mind by your own thoughts and you'll be better equipped to hear what is truly being said. Oftentimes, we place a dark filter on others and we hear their words through the dark filters that we have created in our minds about them. If you really believe that your spouse, coworker, or boss is completely wrong in all that they say, or do, then re-evaluate that notion. Question your own thoughts and feelings about whoever you think your enemy is. Jesus Christ said, "The lamp of the body is the eye. If therefore your eye is good, your whole body will be full of light. But if your eye is bad, your whole body will be full of darkness. If therefore the light that is in you is darkness, how great is that darkness!" (Matthew 6:22-23, NKJV). We see and hear others through the filters we have created in our minds. Clean out the clutter in your own mind, then you can discern the good from the evil in another.

3) The lack of self-control also exemplifies itself in rudeness.

We cut people off with our cars and our words. Our desire to control our lanes, our safety, and our time takes precedence over civility. Your time is not more important than others. Stop being late to meetings, it's rude. Stop cutting people off with your vehicle just because you can, or, because you left late, and now you want to take it out on other people. Refuse to be mean. Stop trying to win every argument, or debate. Examine yourself. Ask yourself, "Why am I so angry right now? Why am I engaging this person in debate? Why am I in this rush? Why did I just rudely interrupt this person again? What am I hoping to gain by cursing, or verbally assaulting this person?" Stop the mandate that you are the most important person around. Stop the cursing. Stop the verbal assaults. They are toxic to the other person and to you. Stop it. Breathe and breathe again. Remain silent when you need to be silent. To everything there is a season. Perhaps the season of silence has reached your mind and peace is on your horizon.

4) This leads us to another trait of the lack of self-control – not knowing when to be quiet or when to cease from arguing. When your conversation, or disagreement, continues into nagging, badgering, or completely tearing into another person verbally, simply because "you could not help yourself"; you're out of control. You *can* help yourself. You have to face that fact that you *can* help yourself and others by being able to know *when enough is enough.* The jerk may possibly continue down a path where violence could occur because he/she refuses to cooperate and stop talking when the need arises. I've often wondered how many times we have watched the news and they say that so and so left the scene of an argument and came back and

shot the person they were arguing with, or, that a knife or gun was pulled and used as a result of an escalated argument. Dear jerk, in your all-knowing mind, do you propose to know when enough has been enough so that you can continue your rage, uncaring what their response to your rage might be?

People who live in the moment of their expressions, disregarding the affect they might have on another, will most likely live to regret those expressions. "I wish I hadn't said...I wish I hadn't done that," are often "wishes" after the pain has been inflicted, and the wounds cannot be undone. We can be assured of reactions to our actions.

Watch to understand the reactions of others. Your words will enlarge and encourage, exalt and applaud, be positive and uplifting...or, they will inflict pain, negativity, remorse, and guilt, as well as, be mean-spirited, abusive, or vile. Our words matter to others. Our actions and behaviors matter to others. Our words and actions create reactions. We cannot control others actions, what they think, or how they think. We cannot control another person's reactions either. If we speak in positive terms, hopefully, we are received with positivity. If we speak in negative terms, we can be guaranteed it will be received with negative connotations.

One afternoon as I was teaching a class, Joey had come in and sat by himself at the edge of one of the sets of tables. There were two sets of tables. Many of the boys sat at one set of tables and a diverse group of students sat at the other. It seemed to me that Joey wanted to be a part of the boys' group and yet, there was this angst between him and Donovan. Donovan was the leader, of sorts, of the boys, and Joey was constantly berated Donovan for everything that he did. Joey not only annoyed Donovan with his badgering, he annoyed the other boys, as well and when he wasn't successful annoying the boys, he would turn his attention to the other group of students and start complaining about what they were doing wrong. Mind you, Joey had not even begun his schoolwork, nor had completed anything he was told to do. He paid me no mind until, as I was substituting at the time, I asked him his name and went back to my desk and began writing things down on a piece of paper.

Joey was intrigued by what I was writing, so he got up to view what I was writing and I immediately flipped the paper over so he could not see. His obvious interest in my writing quieted him and he went back to his seat and sat down. I smiled inside, turned the paper over and wrote some more. One thing that I wrote was that Joey had isolated himself from the other students voluntarily and out of his great need for attention, constantly berated the other students in order to get their attention. His behavior alienated himself from them and yet, he did not understand that. The more I wrote, the more Joey was intrigued.

Joey, on his own, got up and walked his backpack over beside another student and joined in with the diverse group of students, who were mostly female. However, even with this move, he was still berating Donovan for any move that he might make. Finally, Joey screamed out, "Mr. Lursen, Donovan just showed me his middle finger!" I did not see what Joey saw, but had been listening to the retorts back and forth between the two.

I responded, "Joey, you started this argument. You have constantly complained about everything since you've been in here. You need to have self-control and stop picking on the other students."

After that, Joey seemed to catch a glimpse of understanding. He knew that I was telling the truth. The rest of the class time was quiet for everyone.

It seemed that Joey was obviously being left out, but it was as a result of his own lack of self-control. Many of his ugly comments were something about how the other students were acting and he was directly rebuking them for supposedly disturbing others, when he was the main culprit in the disruption.

What I want us to see here is this: the person who most desires to control others is the very same person who has the least amount of self-control. This is not always the case of every manager, CEO, or parent, but it happens enough that we must take note of it. What we often see are people who want to control others, but lack the concept of self-control themselves. It is the proverbial out of control person telling other people what to do and they're mean-spirited about it. The fascinating thing about this is that the out of control person does not see their own lack of self-control while they are in their glory of attempting to control other people. It is as though they look into a mirror and immediately forget what they just saw.

One other thing, stop bullying yourself by not forgiving yourself for the things that you've done, or said. You cannot go back in time and change any of the decisions you've made in your life, but you can change your future through forgiveness of yourself. I owned a Christian bookstore years ago and one morning a woman that I had known to be a neighbor in the community where we lived was there to meet me as I opened up the door that morning. She was crying. I had known her to be a drug addict and an alcoholic and she had moved out of her home of a husband and three children. She kind of went awol for a while and no one knew what she had done.

Through her tears, she confessed to me that she was so happy for me that I had started up the Christian bookstore and that she was proud of me for doing so. Then, she told me that she had been in some type of rehab and was trying to get her life back together, but she couldn't let go of all that she had done to her children. We prayed together as we had in times past. I found out a month later that she had committed suicide. Learn to forgive others, learn to forgive yourself.

If, after all of these directions, suggestions and imperatives, you find that you cannot identify with making changes, then, purchase Life Coach Mike Bayer's book entitled, "**Best Self: Be You, Only Better**". I have observed Mike Bayer on the Dr. Phil show and he has this particular technique of listing the attributes of your best self…who you believe you are when you are acting your best self. Then, you list the horrible aspects of your life…not things you've done, but the really bad character traits of who you have been through the years, "your anti-self". The person is to take these two lists and decide who they really want to be. When we are honest with ourselves and we write down these horrible character traits, we see ourselves naked, and one by one, with time and help, we can begin to work these traits out of our lives.

Chapter 9

How to Make Better Decisions

I am discovering in this life that the most important, or the most valuable, thing you can teach a child is how to make a wise decision. I asked someone what they thought was the most important thing you could teach a child and she said, "To love." I referred her to the proverb, "Train up a child in the way he should go and he will not depart from it." (Pro. 22:6). It is to say that if you teach a child to make wise decisions, the right decisions, the right pathway, the ethical, the moral, and the spiritual pathway, they will, indeed, find love because they will have been taught to make the most-wise decisions possible along the way. This way leads to peace, love and joy in the Holy Spirit with God in His kingdom.

Decisions are not just made every day, decisions are made in every moment of every day. We decide every moment what to think in that moment; what to say, or, not to say...we decide. It is the immature and irresponsible that blame others for their decisions. The "not me", the "it's somebody else's fault", the "I didn't do it" generation is alive and well today, as it has been for centuries.

We make decisions for self, for others, for our children, for our spouses, our friends, and our enemies. We make decisions regarding our finances, our jobs, our businesses, our social standing, our speech, our tone, and our emotional and mental state and it is all derived from our very own thought processes.

Our decisions come from and are made from our own internal thoughts. "As a man thinks in his heart, so is he..." (Pro. 23:7, ESV). If we spend our time thinking about our fears and worries, then our emotional state is going to be filled with despair and hopelessness, which will influence how we view our world, which, in turn affects the momentary decisions that we make. I knew a woman whose house had been broken into and some of her most prized possessions were stolen. The thieves, who happened to have broken into many homes in the area, were eventually caught and imprisoned. Yet, this poor woman was afraid to leave her house out of fear that someone else would break into her home and steal the other prized possessions that had been secretly hidden. If she did leave her home, it was only for short trips and no longer than a few hours. She was imprisoned in her own home, in her own mind, and she made decisions every day, believing with her whole heart that someone else was coming into her home and stealing things. As her life turned into years, it did come to light that her own adult daughter was taking things from her every time she came to visit her.

Her fears were realized by experience. I am not one to say that her fears caused her daughter to steal her possessions, that is foolishness for the daughter was a thief, but I can see where the beginning of her fears grew in her mind and were reinforced over time by her daughter's actions.

If we live with anger in our thoughts, our emotional state will grow to be antagonistic towards just about everybody. The vicious tone of voice will abound on the inside and any time the supposition of conflict arises, the angry tiger will lash out...sometimes for apparently no reason to the people that surround this internally angry person.

Terry E. Lursen

You control what you think.
You alone are in charge of your thoughts.

If we are constantly thinking about our past and those awful things we did, it will seep out as sludge to others. Sometimes we live in embarrassment and humiliation at some of the things we have said, or done. Constant and unrelenting introspection into the horrible decisions of our past will eventually lead our emotional state to fretful regret, humiliating despair, and a miserable view of life. If we think on these things, our conversations will typically be depressing, negative and pessimistic. We will become the least likely person in the room to be asked, "How are you doing?" because the people that care about you the most will already know that if they ask, something ugly, negative, or mean-spirited will come out of our mouths...because that is just how we think. The person who dwells in self-pity and regret lives in a pool of excessive darkness and gets so comfortable with it that when they start talking about their lives, they really believe that the dark swirl is visible to others, when, in actuality, the dark swirl only dwells in the person's mind and comes out of their mouths when they are invited to talk. People need agreement with their thoughts, and if they cannot find someone to agree with them, they will talk themselves into an agreed state of defilement. We all know various people that we are quite neglectful to when it comes to asking them, "How are you doing?" because we "don't want to go there with them" sadly enough. We decide every moment what we think about. We have the God given ability to say, "No!' to every errant thought.

Self-introspection is one thing and harboring an unforgiving spirit is another. I know of people who wake up every morning angry at the world. They awake to their anger, that inner tiger, constantly ruminating on past events and people who they blame for ruining their lives, ruining their work life, or ruining their day yesterday. They refuse to let the anger go and their anger gets fed throughout the day with one thought after another.

Whatever you feed, becomes stronger.
Choose to identify the anger triggers.

The thoughts coming from something, or someone, who may not have had anything to do with your past, yet, they trigger the tiger. You are in charge of your thoughts, not the trigger, not the other person, or thing. You choose your thoughts. Stop your own madness of blaming others for your emotions.

Learn to say, "No!" to errant thoughts.

Hopefully, this discussion will lead us to realize that we cannot change our past. Every decision that we make gets locked in the past. Once a momentary decision is made in the present, the decision just made and turned into action becomes locked in the past; if only just a thought, the principle is still the same. We train our minds and follow the railroad tracks that we have laid down in our constant and unabated relishing of stuck thinking. We do not take action on every thought, thank God; at least we are not supposed to. We are to think through the dilemmas of the day, however, simply thinking through something thoroughly is not the same as dwelling in a well of grudgeful regret, as well as, making the final decision.

It is those final decisions that we made in those moments that are locked in our past. We cannot go back and retrieve them and unlock the long chain of decisions that we made fifty, forty, or thirty years ago, or even thirty minutes ago. We can make new, more thought out, decisions, but we cannot undo what we did back then, some time in our past. The decisions are locked in the annals of time and nothing can be done about it. This is the inherent problem with divorce. A person believes differently now about their partner and figures that a divorce will undo what they have done, so they seek to be free. Once a person has known, in the Biblical sense, another person and have been made one in the eyes of God, no person can undo that, even with the writ of divorce.

We can decide in our present and that affects our future, but we cannot undecide a decision in our past. The adult who has made horrible and regretful decisions in the past has to accept responsibility for their decisions, but that does not mean living in a cesspool of regret in the corner of a room where they are afraid to make any more decisions because their past is being allowed to rule their present with unrelenting fervor. Some folk sit in a room alone when they get old and are stifled by a demon in their minds that is constantly hitting them over the head with a battering ram of remorse demanding that they not move, or decide, any more decisions, out of guilt, shame and tragic hopelessness. This should not be.

I often find it amusing each time we receive a mutual fund prospectus and, although the fund has had super growth in the past, the prospectuses will always say in the fine print, "past performance does not guarantee future success." Your past does not guarantee the success, or failure, of your future. What does affect your future are your present decisions. Accept the truth of your past and know that the interlocked decisions are locked. We cannot unlock them. We have to move on. What we continually have to learn and be reminded of is how to make wise decisions in our present so that when we move about in our future, we are not burdened by the past.

"As a man thinks in his heart, so is he."

The kingdom believer is admonished to "...destroy arguments and every lofty opinion raised against the knowledge of God, and take every thought captive to the obedience of Christ..." (2 Cor. 10:5, ESV). We choose to think what we think. If we dwell in thoughts of positive peace, joy, and abounding love, our emotional state will lead us to decisions based on hopefulness, understanding, and loving fruitfulness. I speak the truth here. False prophets get in the way here and say that if you will think positive thoughts of peace, love and joy, you'll get blessings, called money, cars and houses. That is not in the Bible anywhere. What I'm saying is if you will fill your days with thoughts of cheerfulness, positivity, peace, love and joy, those things will emanate from you heart...cheerfulness, positivity, peace, love, and joy. Your words will follow what is in your heart. Your decisions will find themselves waiting to be made because impertinence and grieving impatience do not dwell with kindness, gentleness, perseverance, and patience. Light overcomes darkness. If we say we live in the light, then we should be walking in the light.

Jesus said, "For where your treasure is, there your heart will be also. The eye is the lamp of the body. If your vision is clear, your whole body will be full of light. But if your vision is poor, your whole body will be full of darkness. If then the light within you is darkness, how great is that darkness." (Matt. 6:21-23, Berean Study Bible).

The mind of man is like a prism. A prism is a glass or other transparent object in prism form, especially one that is triangular with refracting surfaces at an acute angle with each other and that separates white light into a spectrum of colors. When light passes through a prism the light bends. As a result, the different colors that make up white light become separated. This happens because each color has a particular wavelength and each wavelength bends at a different angle. A scientist can direct a spectacular beam of bright, white light through a prism, and because of the angles of the prism, the white light that passes through bends and reveals the different colors that make up white, presumably red, green, and blue.

Again, the mind of man is like a prism. Perfect wisdom, factual information, or simple knowledge can go into one person's mind and depending on the angles (the person's own perceptions, experiences, intellectual understanding, spiritual revelation, education levels and the such) the wisdom, factual information, and knowledge will pass through this prism and the person will arrive at a particular belief(s). The same wisdom, factual information, and knowledge can pass into and through another person's mind, or prism, and that person, because of their prism angles (the person's own perceptions, experiences, intellectual understanding, spiritual revelation, education levels and the such) that person can arrive at completely different ideas, or beliefs than the other person. The input can be the same, but the individual mind, refracts the information into colors of their own mind. "The eye is the lamp (prism/mind) of the body. If your vision is clear, your whole body will be full of light. But if your vision is poor, your whole body will be full of darkness. If then the light within you is darkness, how great is that darkness." (Matt. 6:22-23, Berean Study Bible). How you see a thing will be how that thing is dispersed in and through your mind. This is how the truth becomes a lie in the eyes of darkness versus the eyes that search for truth and hold it dear to their hearts. This is also why Dr. Phil McGraw consistently says, "Perception is reality." It may not be the Truth, but it is your reality. Thus, how you see a thing is how you will think and reflect on whatever has been proposed to you, whether it has come from knowledge, love, or a perceived enemy. You will decide and make your further decisions based on what you have thought through. The basic tenet to making the best decision is to think, to think rightly, to think rightly through the decision and weigh all of the options that are within your reach. Research the options and analyze the research. If you are a praying person, pray for direction. Seek direction and advice. I have learned to ask the family first, "What do you think about this particular project?" I respect all of them, we are a family team.

This is why I believe that the most important thing that you can teach a child is how to make a wise decision. In teaching the value of making wise decisions, we are teaching children how to think through a thing before they come to any type of decision. We are building a child's prism, their mind in how they see things, from the day of their birth until they get away from us and begin teaching others what and how they think. If we can teach a child how to make a decision, we can teach ourselves as well.

If the parent is impetuous, rash, and irrational, then, the parent is directly, indirectly and in every virtual way, teaching their child to be as they are. Parents model what they are every moment of every day. If there are no consequences to the parents' behavior, the child will think that value belongs to them as well. If a husband, or wife, is a bully to their spouse, or to the children, the children will learn to hate bullies and in so doing, become, from reflecting traits and behavior, the very thing that they hate and hate will fill their hearts with anguish that will not go away simply because a bigger bully has pushed them down, or worse. Little bullies can grow up to be royal jerks.

"Train a child in the way they should go, and when he is old, he will not depart from it." Proverbs 22:6

Teaching a child to make right-wise decisions involves:
1) A responsible, maturing adult that knows the difference between right and wrong. The Ten Commandments is the first place to start. (Exodus 20)
2) A responsible, maturing adult who is learning to be patient, kind, loving, disciplined, and intuitive.
3) A responsible, maturing adult who really cares about the child and their well-being. When the parent cares, the child will follow suit.
4) A responsible, maturing adult who understands that creating a standard of ethical and moral behavior in the home begins first, second, and third with the parent exemplifying the standards of behavior first and teaching them directly to the child in a loving and disciplined manner.
5) Helping the child to understand through practice, what is right from wrong; what is acceptable and what is not.
6) Teaching the child to do, and say, to others what they would have others do, and say, to them.
7) Teach the child to think before acting. This takes copious amounts of time with the parent being with the child and is a parental responsibility.
8) Practice discipline at the grocery store, the department store and at other venues where the child enjoys seeing something, or wanting something that they simply cannot have, or, do not need.
9) Teach the difference between needs, wants, and desires. Teach financial concepts that involve the discipline of pa-

tience and appropriation. (ie., the family needs food at the grocery store before we go and buy another pair of tennis shoes, a toy, your favorite candy bar, or soda drink).

This is simply the place to start. One could go online and see the plethora of ideas on how to teach children. Even though every family is different, the basic fundamentals of ethics and morals taught in the Bible stories are imperative for raising up a child in the way that they should go. The parent must be fully conscious that everything they do and say is being taught to the child. Words, tone, actions, behaviors, expenditures, the ways and means to accomplishing and completing tasks all are watched with searching eyes on how Dad, or Mom, did, or said a thing. We are living proof that children learn to be like their parents and teachers. We hear it in our voices, our words and in our actions. We will see it in our adult children and, hopefully what you see and hear in your adult children will be pleasing to your eyes and ears and will also be pleasing to the eyes and ears of a Holy God.

Chapter 10

Thinking About How Other People Think

"As a man thinks in his heart, so is he..." is a quote from Jesus Christ. Jesus also said, "Pass no judgment and you will not be judged. For as you judge others, you will yourselves be judged, and whatever measure you deal out to others will be dealt back to you." (Matthew 7:1-2, New English Bible).

We get hung up on others' words, dispositions, tone of voice, moods and behaviors and, we judge them according to these things...their words, their tone of voice, their disposition, their moods, and their behaviors. We judge them according to how we think. If we happen to agree with the person, then, in our opinion, they say, or act appropriately. If we happen to disagree, or, simply not like the person, then, in our opinions, they cannot do right, say right, or the very least we say to them, "It's not what you said, it's how you said it." Then, we go off on them as to how wrong they are, or, we just go off away from them, not to be burdened by their presence.

Sometimes we think another person is being the bully, the jerk, the stupid, or the idiot, when it's really us not understanding how they think and then, they come across to us as unthinking, unkind, uncaring, and all round unintelligent. I am here to tell you that the majority of people do not think like you think. You may have found yourself happy in your group with people who think what you think, but I guarantee you that even though others may think, or believe **what** you think, or believe, they arrived at the same conclusion differently than you did. There is a considerable difference in **what** people think and **how** people think. We need to arrive at a place in our lives where we can exchange ideas through dialogue and not be hateful in our speech for it leads us to harm others with piercing words as well as it leads us to harm ourselves causing personal alienation and isolation.

Again, we mistakenly and inadvertently judge others on their words and behaviors, when we should not be doing anything of the sort, because we don't have the whole picture. To be certain, there are those who misquote and misuse, to the point of ignorant abuse, this Jesus principle thinking that we cannot think anything about another and that is not the context of what Jesus was talking about here. In this context, Jesus was talking about mercy and how it is not our responsibility to form judgments about other people. In other places of scripture, Jesus clearly tells His disciples to discern the good from the bad, particularly as it relates to our leaders. There are bad people who display their badness by their words, by their behaviors, and as Jesus explicitly told His disciples…observe their fruit, their fruit comes from within, as it does with all of us… as a man thinks in his heart, so he will speak, act, and display fruit whose root is on the inside of the man, or woman.

To not judge, then, doesn't have anything to do with, "Don't discern, don't think, don't look, don't observe" others, for it has much deeper connotation than thinking and discernment, it has to do with all knowing authority. God is our judge. God is authority. God knows all. We can see the fruit that others display, but we do not know what God knows, their heart, their innermost thoughts, their past, their present, and future. We simply do not know these things and we need to learn to stop passing judgment, particularly, on a person's future, because we do not know. We cannot pass judgment on others because the authority to do so is not ours to take. We do not have the authority in heaven, or on earth, to say a person is a "thus and so" just because we believe it to be true.

Again, we can observe, watch their fruit, their words and behaviors and easily see what is right and what is wrong, but to send someone to hell is not our place. Nor, is it our place to call them out as having a personality disorder because we think they display certain tendencies and proclivities that seem to corroborate what we have read on an internet website.

This brings us to, temporarily, to what I call "The Art of Judging Other People". In my observations of hundreds of people in tens of thousands of conversations, I see trends in the analysis of what people do to others, as well as, what people have done to me. I also see through introspection the processes that my own mind has played through in order to inadequately and unlawfully judge another person.

Generally, people create lines of expectations, also known as, standards, regarding themselves and others. There are very specific things that people expect of themselves and then, what people do is turn around and place their personal self-expectations onto others. These overlaid expectations can either be the same, similar, or completely different lines of expectations. Everyone that I know does this. Unmet expectations lead to frustration in our personal lives. However, when other people do not live up to the expectations that we have secretly, covertly, or openly, placed upon them, it leads to inward, unobjective analysis in our own brains. We may say something to the individual, we may not, but we observe and judge based on what we just saw, or heard.

When we observe another person, in their words/deeds, we assimilate what we believe they've said, or done, from our perspective. We then place those words/deeds into the cauldron called our heart and set them against our own personal lines of expectations of what we would have said, what we would have done, or what Jesus would have said, or done, or your Mama, or whoever. Our lines of expectations that we covertly place on others has a standard that we personally hold dear. For some, it may be their Dad, their pastor/priest, the Bible, some other religion, or their dog, depending just how high their expectations seem to be.

When the other person's words/deeds do not line up with our expectations, or standards, of them, conclusions are immediately formulated in the mind. Judging others is a process, however, the process can take only milliseconds to perform. The process of judging others involves, but, is not limited to: creating our own personal expectations/standards to live by, observing others, comparing the others' words/deeds/standards to our personal standards, forming a pre-conclusion according to the comparison, possibly talking to others (through gossip or seeking another witness) about the other persons' inability to meet our secret expectations, and, then, thinking through and voicing a conclusion, which, for all practical purposes is a judgment either for, or, most likely, against the person we are judging.

All of this process can take mere moments because we are seeing, or hearing these words and deeds from our perspective and we judge others based on this perspective.

People judge other people every day...all day long, and most of the time, they don't even know they're doing it.

I want to propose an element to this theory of the Art of Judging Others and that is how and why some people are judged differently than others:

> **People do not judge people that they like,**
> **they give them a free of judgment pass.**
>
> **Most people who judge people judge people**
> **that they don't like,**
> **people with unshared beliefs,**
> **people who are different than they are.**

Do you believe that these statements are true? Do you believe that it is true of you? I believe that it is true of everyone, whether you believe, or not. We inherently judge others based on how we feel about them especially when we do not know that we do it.

The people that you care about the most, you do not judge with the same standards as, let's say, someone that has antithetical beliefs to you, or, perhaps, in your mind, you despise a person based on what they look like, how they smell, how they dress, the food they eat, the car they drive, the money, or the lack of money that they possess, their possessions, their belief systems, their religion, their sex, their intelligence, or the lack thereof. There are thousands of reasons that we can find to see other people as different than ourselves and *we judge them based on the distance of the difference.*

Birds of a feather flock together and even if both of you are drunkards and penniless, you have a tendency not to judge the person who seems to be just like you. But, when it comes to other people who are different, you know, the ones that you hate, despise, do not care about and cannot stand to hear them talk, or breathe...you castigate with the sword in your heart and tear them down unmercifully without saying a word...all done in your heart, the throne room of judgment.

The people least likely to get judged by you are those people that you love, respect, honor, care for and tolerate so you give them allowances. These people that you tolerate with love and admiration can be complete turds of the human race, but they think and act and believe what you believe, so, they are good with you. The same is true for people that like what we like. We tend to like people who like what we like and do not hold them accountable as we do the other folk who do not agree with us.

The people that you are most likely to judge are those that you treat with disdain, you disrespect them, and keep a critical disposition while you are around them, or, thinking of them. Vituperative attacks are bitter and abusive. There are many reasons why Jesus said, "Do not judge, for ever how you judge is how you will be judged."

Typically, people know when they are being judged. They may say something, in return, they may not. Oftentimes, people (the victims) are shocked by our judgments. That's when we have exhibited ourselves to be critical, judgmental, voicing our cruel opinions of them, what they wear, how they talk, what they've said, what they've done, or not done, etc. This is how and when we play the bully, the jerk, to others by our judgements against them. People do it every day, all day long. Harsh judgments formed in the heart seethe to overflow against our perceived ideological enemies. We hear the opprobrious words of "stupid, idiot, narcissist, ignorant, and deplorable" with the intent to be condescending, scornful and denigrating.

The U.S. Forest Service, back in the 1940's through the 60's, had a phrase by Smokey the Bear that stated, "Only you can prevent forest fires." In kind, only you can stop the harsh judgments in your heart that can lead to more denigrating and cruel words and deeds.

In speaking with a friend, she noted how great the difference in her thinking became after she came to a new group of people that actually knew how to love people. She came to experience Christ Jesus that was very similar to the day that she met Jesus for the first time. Years ago, after she believed that she had been born again, she got into the church and there, things seemed very different than her personal experience of Christ. As she matured into an adult, life happened, and she became more cynical in the religious system. Over the years, her personal message became negative and judgmental. She believed that she was not experiencing the true, authentic love of Christ. From her perspective, the leaderships' lives did not line up with what they were preaching and she confronted them about it. She felt like she was being used for the leadership's benefit as their ulterior motives were being revealed to her. Now, she is free from negative, judgmental thinking because she has been holy loved by others into wholeness.

As we continue to grow in our thinking, and in our mercy, we learn that others not only think differently than what we think, but they think differently in how we think. Deductively thinking is, "a process of reasoning from one, or more statements (premises) to reach a logically certain conclusion. It links premises with the conclusions. In this, if the premises are true, the terms are clear and the rules of deductive logic are followed, then the conclusion reached is necessarily true."[12] We tend to think deductively when the obvious is the best conclusion. Not everyone thinks deductively, or even cares to think this way, especially in our current philo-

---

[12] Usage notes, Dictionary.com

sophical and ideological environment.

In inductive reasoning, the person, thinker, or scientist, is after is the possibility, or probability, rather than the truth, or certainty. They want options in what could be, as opposed to the definitive. Then, they can take these options, or best educated guess and put them through a deductive process to find the truth in the matter... or not. It is taking past experiences and making future predictions. Its effort is put towards what is most likely in order to eliminate what isn't true, or, likely. Sometimes, the thinker stops at their conclusion and the truth of it doesn't matter; they believe their conclusion, or, they believe their conclusion to be true, even though, in truth, it isn't. They either do not know that it's not true, or, they do not care that it's not true, for what they are after is the process to get to the possibilities, or highest probability.

You can easily see where arguments could ensue between a deductive thinking person and an inductive thinking person where both believe that their conclusion is true. If a person happens to be a "name-caller" or a swearing person, then it takes little time for them to start with their epithets and what is really happening is that the two people think differently on how to arrive at a particular conclusion, with both parties presuming that their version of the truth is truer than the other's. It is possible for a deductive argument that is logically valid, but is not sound. Fallacious arguments often take that form.[213]

A valid premise is merely a premise to discuss the case at hand, it can be true, or not. A sound conclusion is a conclusion where both the premises are true and the conclusion is also true...that's what makes a "sound" argument.

Have you ever argued with a person who was arguing just for the sake of arguing? They had no intention of winning or losing

---

[13] International Encyclopedia of Philosophy www.iep.utm.edu

the debate, they just wanted to be heard. To the one, the argument had no basis, or truth in the case, but to the other, that didn't matter. Sometimes folk just need to talk because...just because. And, if you care about that person, they will eventually get around to why they're talking, or debating. They are struggling to be heard and do not know any other way to get our attention.

Not only is there deductive and inductive reasoning, there is also abductive reasoning. "The abductive thinker infers, guesses, and seeks the simplest and most likely explanation to the thought process and their conclusions do not necessarily verify the truth. It is based on testing a hypothesis using the best possible information available. It often entails making an educated guess after observing phenomena for which there is no clear explanation. It is often used for forming hypotheses to be tested. Examples of this type of reasoning are doctors who make diagnosis based on test results and by jurors who make decisions based on the evidence presented to them."3[14]

Abductive reasoning involves drawing a conclusion based on the explanation that best explains a state of events, rather than by evidence provided by the premises. Inference to the best explanation.4[15]

To the abductive thinker, it is imperative to do the most research, get the most data possible, and to make certain that the most data is the most factual, so that the proposed conclusions drawn from the data is the best possible solution. It is why doctors run those tests and it is also what drives me to think outside the boxes of time and space to attempt to figure out why we do what we do so that we can stop doing the things that we do that harm us. Sometimes, the things we hear from the pulpit are not true,

---

[14] Wikipedia.org deductive/abductive

[15] ibid.

nor are most things that we hear coming from Washington, DC, or, the media. For some reason, or, lack of reasoning, the speakers stopped short with their investigating analysis and came upon something they could believe in, or suited them best, rather than facts, or the absolute truth.

At times, we may reason deductively to make one decision and think abductively to make another. Hopefully, our desire is to make the best decision possible with the best, possible information available which, in principle, would be proven evidence that is testable and factual. It is the conclusions that we reach where we find the most turmoil in getting along in our relationships. Husbands and wives don't always arrive at the same conclusions and if they do, it may have been from different processes in reasoning. One person may have guessed the same conclusion as me and I think we are on the same page and yet, I find out that we are nothing of the same when it comes to a different problem because that person does not think as I think. That does not make me right, it simply makes us different. I don't always think and process in the same ways. I discovered that, at times, I will, mistakenly, argue a conclusion that has not been conclusively proven true. I will argue from what I believe to be the best possible explanation, which is a part of the scope of abductive reasoning. My desire is to get to the truth of the matter. I'm not always successful, yet I am learning not to be a jerk in the process of debate.

Occam's razor is a problem-solving principle that states, "Entities should not be multiplied without necessity." In other words, the simplest solution is usually the right one. (Wikipedia).

When conclusions, though, are drawn from preconceived ideas, we all run into the miry clay of the unexplainable. Once we get a notion that something is absolutely true, it is practically impossible for someone else to get us to un-believe our beliefs. We border on the delusional if we refuse to listen to others when they are telling us the truth about ourselves and we deny, deny, deny because of our own self-deception.

What is true? It is what it is, or, things aren't what they seem?

So, what is the point of all of this talk of differing types of reasoning? It is **how** people think that gets them to **what** they think. If you find yourself talking, or, arguing, with another person and you see them as, perhaps, the most unreasonable person on earth, then, think again. Perhaps their conclusion came about from a perfectly rational view that you had not thought of, or, maybe, just maybe, you haven't thought through to the end of a matter and the other person has. Is it typical for one person to be right and the other wrong in the process of debate? Or, is it possible for both of you to be wrong, or, both of you to be right, or, both of you have true and/or false premises and a compromise is all you can arrive at for the moment? It is Ok to table a disagreement until another time so that both of you can do more research, or, to give more time to what the other person is saying. No one wants to be around the impossible person...the impossible person, in this context, the jerk, is the one who thinks he/she is right, always and forever, or even most of the time. The impossible person is likely acting like a jerk and no one wants to be around that person. If you find yourself alone, maybe it isn't all because you chose to be alone. It could be that you have drowned out all of the possibilities of thought that are different than yours and here you are, alone again...naturally.

Chapter 11

Final Words

In Galatians 5, the Bible talks about the fruit of the Spirit, which is love, joy, peace, patience, goodness, kindness, gentleness, faithfulness and self-control.

What we oftentimes see at church, at home, in the marketplace, or at school, is the complete opposite. Where there should be love, we sense hate, or a hateful spirit and the tongue is ensued. Where there should be joy, unhappy people try to make the other people around them as unhappy as they are. Where there should be peace, discord and division reign.

Where there should be patience, impatience, rudeness and demanding imperativeness is exemplified.

Where there should be goodness, coarseness, bad-temper, and ugly tones of voice are screaming for attention.

Where there should be kindness, a mean spirit is prevailing.

Where there should be faithfulness, which is being true to one's word, or devoted to one's duty, there is disloyalty, deceptiveness, and lying.

And, where there should be self-control, which is the ability to have control over one's will, emotions, words, and actions, there is the polar opposite...the imbalanced life, lacking planning, undisciplined, excessive in most things that they do, addictive personalities to substances, power, money, fame, or their own personalities.

The people lacking self-control are out to gratify themselves first, second, and third. Dr. Les Carter[11] stated that the imperative person is often overwhelmed by his own importance. Don't be that guy who doesn't see his own hypocrisy when he is standing before a crowd, trying to tell people how they should live and, yet, his own belly protrudes over his beltline because of all of the fried chicken, ice cream and diet drinks he, or she, consumes daily.

Let's not make this too difficult. If you find yourself doing these mean-spirited things, then, do the opposite. From your own heart choose to be loving, be kind, be good, be gentle, talk with a gentle voice. I started with calling my dogs using French. It's a softer language.

If you possess that mean tone of voice, take control over that bad habit, by speaking with a gentle voice. Get rest every day. Remove the anger, that resentful tiger, from your life. Stop living at a stress level 10. People will love you for it, rather than shunning you and desiring to leave your presence.

Learn to do the opposite of "taking control" over people. What is the opposite? Mercy. Learn to love mercy, for in your days you will see the need for it. Learn to give mercy, for in your future, you will desire it most of all when you die. Learn to be merciful, for in being merciful, we reap mercy in the law of sowing and reaping. Allow others to be who they are.

Mercy moves towards the needs of people, control doesn't care about others' needs, it only cares for itself in the moment.

If you have been the victim of the bully or the jerk, refuse to do the in-kind work and serving up your own form of justice. Learn to forgive, learn to walk away, learn to redirect, to not focus on what they've done, or said, and chart a new course. My daughter, Jessica, once told me, "Don't get offended, just go in a different direction."

While watching America's Got Talent this summer, there was

a young teenage contestant that wrote and sang her own original song. It was about being bullied. After her subsequent performance of singing another song, Simon Cowell, one of the well-known judges said to her, "You sang a song once about being bullied. I don't want you to think about them anymore. Don't give them power over you. You take power over you. Forget about them and move on. I'm speaking to you as a father, I don't want to hear about those people here anymore."

There is reasonable expectation in how we treat other people. We reap what we sow. If you call yourself a Christian, it's probably time for your Bible reading to have been absorbed into your spirit so that you are the living word and not a mere memorizer. The Word of God must become life in us in how we treat other people.

I am learning to talk less, listen more intently, and to learn from Paul when he said, "I die daily." This dying daily is an everyday occurrence…everyday, in the moment by moment. I have to guard my heart, guard my tongue, my tone, and my own disposition. I have to seek peace, and pursue it, so that I am able to walk in peace.

How can I offer peace to someone if I have none to give?

We all reap what we sow in this life or in the next. We may not see our vile words spoken and the pain we have inflicted on others immediately, we may, we may not. We may not see our terrible ways until years later when we are treated with disrespect in an adult child because we continually mistreated their mother, or father, with disdain and disrespect. Words and actions have rewards and consequences. Words do not evaporate into the atmosphere. Words are heard and stored. Words are remembered and kept in vaults of memories as the disposition of the person speaking is heard in the echoes of the mind being played over and over again... rehearsed, only to be played back as your child has now become an adult and they say what you said in a tone that bespeaks of the devil. Understand the reactions of others; it's a valid, and a sound, part of growing up into maturity.

In many ways, we are all farmers. We take what we have in our hands, and in our mouths, and we fling it out into the fields of the human race. We are sowing our seeds every day. You cannot look at your own children and say, "I did not plant that." If you want a different response, you have to change.

Some sow seeds of discontent, discord and division. Some sow seeds of peace, love, and joy. Some sow seeds of perverted desires, abusing even the smallest of children. Some sow seeds of justice, righteousness, and goodwill. And, still others, sow mixed seed of blessing and cursing, confusing the most innocent of children.

We choose what we sow every day.
We cannot say with honesty that others chose for us.

We choose to love, or to hate. We choose to be at peace, or at war. We choose to love and stay committed in faithfulness, or we choose to be unfaithful, loose and immoral. We choose to be offended, instead, we can choose to walk away, or to simply redirect.

We choose what we sow and how we sow it. We reap what we have sown and then, sow it again. The effort then, should be on planting good seed.

Plant good seed with good words and good deeds.
You will reap a harvest of goodness.

Choose to sow love, peace and joy. Choose to walk in self-control, goodness, and gentleness. Choose to be faithful when the world says to follow the road to perdition. Choose to be kind, full of patience, yes, that's it...choose to be kind and patient. And the seed that you sow will come back to you, some in multiples too numerous to count.

If you want to be respected, respect others.

If you want to be loved, love other people.

If you want to be treated with kindness, be kind to others.

If you want to be forgiven, forgive.

If you want to be filled with joy, give...pressed down, shaken together, with all that you have...give, and I pray that what you give in mercy, forgiveness, love, respect, peace and joy is returned to you in multiples of goodness.

In a child, you are creating a work of art.
Every word and every action is a seed and those seeds go into
your children and, vicariously, into other children every day.
The purpose of nature is growth and the seeds you plant will
grow into a harvest of magnificent proportions.

After you are no more,
what mark will you have made on
the children in your world?

References and Citations

Allender, Dr. Dan B., **The Wounded Heart: Hope for Adult Victims of Childhood Sexual Abuse.** Navpress, Colorado Springs, CO. 1995. 1 p. 36

Bayer, Mike, **Best Self: Be You, Only Better**. Dey St. A division of HarperCollins Publishers. New York, New York, 2019.

Carter, Dr. Les. **Imperative People: Those Who Must Be in Control.** Thomas Nelson Publishers, Nashville, TN., 1991.
2 pp. 14,15
3 p. 18
4 p. 19
5 p. 24
6 p. 36

7 Sarkis, Stephanie Moulton, PhD., Psychology Today. https://www.psychologytoday.com/us/blog/here-there-and-everywhere/201201/6-reasons-why-youre-jerk. Copyright 2012 Sarkis Media LLC.

Sarkis, Stephanie, **Gaslighting: Recognize Manipulative and Emotionally Abusive People - And Break Free.** Da Capo Press. New York, New York. 2018.

8 Carter, Dr. Les. Imperative People. p. 21-22.

9 Ortiz, Adam (Jan. 2004). "Cruel and Unusual Punishment: The Juvenile Death Penalty: Adolescence, Brain Development and Legal Culpability". Juvenile Justice Center, American Bar Association.

10 Braiker, Harriet B., PhD. **Lethal Lovers and Poisonous People: How to Protect Your Health from Relationships That Make You Sick**. Pocket Books, Simon & Schuster. New York, New York. 1992. p. 184.

11 Carter, Dr. Les. Imperative People. p. 144.

Machen, J. Gresham, **Christianity & Liberalism**. Wm. B. Eerdmans Publishing Co. Grand Rapids, Michigan. 1923. 2009. p. 110.

New York Post, Andrea Downey, "Brain Scans Reveal How Badly Emotional Abuse Damages Kids." November 2, 2017.

Books Written by
Terry Lursen

The Treasure Within the Kingdom of God
366 daily devotional written according to the Gospel of Jesus Christ, the Kingdom of God - ISBN - 978-0-9910989-0-3

The Looking Glass Water: The Water that Woos - a novel
ISBN - 978-0-9910989-2-7

The Battle for Crested Hill - an allegory
ISBN - 978-0-9910989-5-8

The Dissolution of Truth - a philosophical treatise
ISBN - 978-0-9910989-8-9

www.ingramcontent.com/pod-product-compliance
Lightning Source LLC
Chambersburg PA
CBHW060403080526
44583CB00012B/452